Routledge Revivals

The Opposite Sexes

Originally published in English in 1927, this study discusses the physical differences between men and women and how this affected the often negative views of women of society. With all known information at the time, the author also details perceived mental differences between the sexes and finishes with a brief cultural history of women's place in society. This title will be of interest to students of Gender Studies and History.

The Opposite Sexes
A Study of Woman's Natural and Cultural History

Adolf Heilborn
Translated by
J.E. Pryde-Hughes

First published in 1927
by Methuen & Co. Ltd

This edition first published in 2016 by Routledge
2 Park Square, Milton Park, Abingdon, Oxon, OX14 4RN
and by Routledge
711 Third Avenue, New York, NY 10017

Routledge is an imprint of the Taylor & Francis Group, an informa business

© 1927 Methuen & Co. Ltd

All rights reserved. No part of this book may be reprinted or reproduced or utilised in any form or by any electronic, mechanical, or other means, now known or hereafter invented, including photocopying and recording, or in any information storage or retrieval system, without permission in writing from the publishers.

Publisher's Note
The publisher has gone to great lengths to ensure the quality of this reprint but points out that some imperfections in the original copies may be apparent.

The publishers would like to make it clear that the views and opinions expressed, and language used in the book are the author's own and a reflection of the times in which it was published. No offence is intended in this edition.

Disclaimer
The publisher has made every effort to trace copyright holders and welcomes correspondence from those they have been unable to contact.

ISBN 13: 978-1-138-63879-2 (hbk)
ISBN 13: 978-1-315-63756-3 (ebk)
ISBN 13: 978-1-138-63883-9 (pbk)

THE OPPOSITE SEXES
A STUDY OF WOMAN'S NATURAL AND CULTURAL HISTORY

BY

DR. ADOLF HEILBORN

TRANSLATED FROM THE GERMAN BY

J. E. PRYDE-HUGHES

METHUEN & CO. LTD.
36 ESSEX STREET W.C.
LONDON

First Published in 1927

PRINTED IN GREAT BRITAIN

CONTENTS

CHAP.		PAGE
I	THE PHYSICAL STRUCTURE OF THE FEMALE .	1
II	THE SOUL OF WOMAN	49
III	THE DEVELOPMENT OF THE SOCIAL POSITION OF WOMAN	74

LIST OF ILLUSTRATIONS

FIG.		PAGE
1	EDRIOLYCHNIS SCHMIDTI . . . . (*According to C. Tate Regan and Sámundsson*)	3
2	SHILLUK GIRL, UPPER NILE, WITH TYPICAL KNOCK-KNEES . . . *To face page* Photo: *Prof. Dr. C. Neumann*	14
3	SEX DIFFERENCE IN THE FORMATION OF THE PELVIS	16
4	THE EFFECT OF THE CORSET (4a) The Medici Venus with skeleton sketched in (*according to Sömmering*) (4b) Fashionable lady of the eighteenth century, with skeleton sketched in (*according to Rüdinger*)	19 20
5	SEX DIFFERENCE IN THE SKULL . .	22
6	SEX DIFFERENCE SHOWN IN THE BRAIN OF NEW-BORN CHILDREN . . . . (*According to Rüdinger*)	27
7	FEMALE FIGURE SHOWING STEATOPYGY, CARVED IN STEATITE. AURIGNACIAN: MENTONE CAVE	31
8	THE WILLENDORF VENUS: LIMESTONE STATUETTE. AURIGNACIAN. FROM WILLENDORF, LOWER AUSTRIA . . .	31

viii   THE OPPOSITE SEXES

FIG.		PAGE
9	CLAY FEMALE FIGURE (NEOLITHIC) FROM CUCUTENI, RUMANIA, SHOWING STEATOPYGY . . . . . *To face page*	30
10	FEMALE KORANNA-HOTTENTOT WITH EXAGGERATED STEATOPYGY . . *To face page*	32
11	GIRL FROM THE LOWER NIGER, WITH TYPICAL SMALL HIPS AND CORRESPONDINGLY SMALL, NARROW PELVIS	46
12	HINDOO WIDOW BURNING HERSELF WITH THE CORPSE OF HER HUSBAND . *To face page* (*From "Hindostan" in "The World of Miniature," London, 1822*)	76
13	IDOL OF A PREGNANT WOMAN CUT IN MAMMOTH BONE. AURIGNACIAN, PREDMOST (*Photo: Dr. K. Absolon*) *To face page*	78
14 (*a*)	AGRICULTURAL DIGGING STICK USED BY THE PRESENT-DAY HOTTENTOTS . .	94
14 (*b*)	NUPE-NEGRESS AT WORK IN THE FIELD WITH A HOE	95
15 (*a*)	EGYPTIAN WOMAN WITH SPINDLE SPINNING WHEEL . . . . . *After E. B. Tylor*	96
15 (*b*)	AZTEC GIRL, WEAVING . . . *After E. B Tylor*	96

THE OPPOSITE SEXES

CHAPTER I

THE PHYSICAL STRUCTURE OF THE FEMALE

A BOOK dealing with woman involves some study of man, for man and woman are natural opposites. It is only by opposition and comparison of the two sexes that a sufficiently clear and sharp picture of one and the other can be obtained. The differences revealed may not be so definite as light and shade, or black and white, yet they are distinct enough to be comprehensible. It would seem, further, that each race or folk has the womankind which it deserves, and this indeed applies to every individual male. In other words, the woman to a great degree is the product of man's attitude towards her. It must not be overlooked also that the different sex forms (sex dimorphism, as the biologist says) run down through the whole animal world, and only fail in the lowest organisms.

In this province, nature has occasionally produced singular relations. For instance, there lives in the Southern Seas an extraordinary, greenish-coloured worm, the Bonellia. It is about two to three and a quarter inches long, shaped like a gherkin, and at one end, attached to the 'gherkin' like a stalk, is a forked head, four times as large. This is the female animal, and for a long time only this form was known. But eventually, in the gullet and stomach of the worm another form was found in small colonies of ten to twenty. This was a diminutive, millimetre-long, parasitic creature quite different in shape and colour, and proved to be the corresponding male!

Amongst the Psychidae, a branch of the silkworm family, there are females like fat loathsome caterpillars in appearance, while the males appear as tiny moths. Remy de Gourmont cynically likened the pair to a cow and a cockerel. The female ascendancy is here developed to absurdity.

Even among the vertebrate animals there exist relatively diminutive males. In the class of the arm-finned fish (*Pediculati*), which is very rich in species and includes also the well-known 'Angler' (*Lophius piscatorius*),

PHYSICAL STRUCTURE OF THE FEMALE 3

we find some orders where the grotesque disparity of 'the tiny man and the big wife' is seen in quite an amazing degree. Our first

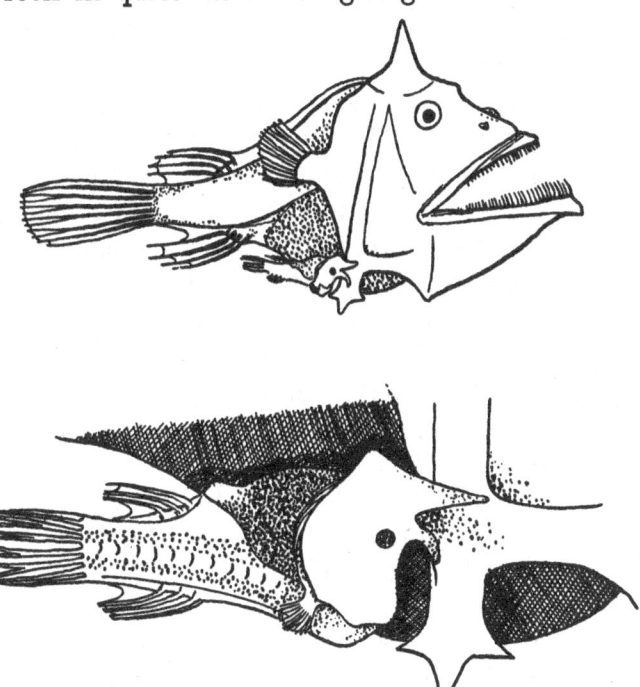

FIG. I.—EDRIOLYCHNIS SCHMIDTI
Above: the female with the male attached behind the gill plates.
Below: the male, much enlarged (according to C. Tate Regan and Sämundsson)

illustration shows the *Edriolychnis schmidti*, living in the Western Atlantic. The tiny male, measuring only 14 mm., is found on the inner side of the female's gill-cover, which is supplied with a three-pointed thorn. The male is seen lying on its back with upturned belly. In the case of the *Ceratius holbölli*, a near relation of the before-mentioned, the female attains to a length of 100 cm., while the male is no longer than 10 cm. From recent important researches by C. Tate Regan, the Director of the Zoological Division of the British Museum, we learn that the male, parasitic on the female, has almost entirely lost his independence. From the female's skin, blood-vessels communicate with those of the male, which is thereby fed. The inner organs of the male are almost entirely stunted. Its body contains scarcely more than the strongly developed genital gland.

Male and female birds are frequently quite different in colour and feather form. For example, the female bird-of-paradise is quite insignificant, while the male flaunts the most wonderful feather forms and colours, the regrettable result of which is that he is sacrificed wholesale in order that his wing and tail feathers may go to decorate the head-dress of European ladies.

The higher the animal stands on the ladder of evolution, the nearer the sexes approach each other in outward aspect. But it is in appearance only, for apart from the manifest

PHYSICAL STRUCTURE OF THE FEMALE 5

difference in the formation of the procreative organs, there are such important anatomical and physiological differences in man and woman that the Danish zoologist, Japetus Steenstrup, was led to declare that 'Sex is not a thing which has its seat in any particular spot, nor does it manifest itself in an especial organ. It operates—and has developed itself —in all parts of the being. The male down to the least part is masculine, no matter how closely he may resemble the female, while in the female the most insignificant part is absolutely female.'

The British anatomist, John Hunter (dec. 1793), and after him, Charles Darwin, described these differences as 'secondary sex characters', without intending to express anything more definite thereby than that these secondary sex indications play a subordinate part in procreation, on which they have only an indirect influence.

Such secondary sex characters are, for example, the development of the antlers of the stag and roe, the 'proboscis' of the male sea-elephant (*Mavrorhinus*), the skin excrescences, folds and combs of reptiles and birds, the mane of the male lion, the stag and the baboon, the beard of man, and numerous other such features which here and there only appear at the rutting period, and are perhaps intended to attract the female.

In all these secondary sex characters the female appears almost invariably to be the primary cause of their production. The British anthropologist, Havelock Ellis, goes still further, and selects still finer ' tertiary ' sex indications (or perhaps more correctly, sex characters of the third rank) which are only apparent when the most searching investigation is made, and an average taken over a long series of individuals.

The differences, anyhow, are indisputable, and in the animal world, as also amongst mankind, we know precisely not just one, but two forms, the male and the female. ' Considered from these two standpoints,' says Rousseau in *Emile*, ' we find so many instances of likeness and unlikeness that it is perhaps one of the greatest of marvels how nature has contrived to make two beings so like and yet so different.' It sounds odd, yet the ' human being ' as distinct from ' man ' and ' woman ' cannot be precisely described in terms of essential qualifications.

In this regard it must be remembered incidentally that—from the extreme standpoint of the too self-conscious ' man '—the assertion has been advanced that woman is anyhow not a human being, a thesis quite clearly revealed in the conclusions of Hippocrates and Aristotle, and which the sixteenth century German humanist and sharp-witted student of Plautus, Acidalius, combated in every way, thereby starting an entertaining discussion at the Council of Macon. Even in modern times we have the spectacle of a famous anatomist, Paul Albrecht, endeavouring, at the Anthropological Meetings at Breslau, 1884, with a great display of scientific learning, to prove the 'greater bestiality' of the female in anatomical respects. Albrecht described woman as being, in several anatomical aspects, much more savage and apelike than the present-day apes, and he maintained, among other things, that 'Proof that the female of the human species is, not only anatomically, but also physiologically the wilder sex, is given by the fact that rarely does man bite or scratch his opponent, while tooth and nail are the favourite weapons of the woman'.

On the other side, there have been many attempts—and not by women alone—to prove exactly the opposite : that the female is the higher developed form of the human being. To my mind the most remarkable of these attempts is the assertion of Ellis, in his comprehensive work *Man and Woman*, that, relatively, the female is notably nearer to the Infant-type, the essential type of the human being, which the adult, in the passage of years, departs from more and more, and that more conspicuously in the case of the man than of the woman.

It is a fact frequently remarked on, that the infant of the anthropoid apes resembles the human being much more closely than does the adult, whose characteristic animal features are more and more evident. 'The ape starts in life with a considerable human endowment,' says Ellis, 'but in the course of life falls far away from it; man starts in life with a still greater portion of human or ultra-human endowment, and to a less extent falls from it in adult life, approaching more and more to the ape. It seems that up to birth, or shortly afterwards, in the higher mammals such as the apes and man, there is a rapid and vigorous movement along the line of upward zoological evolution, but that a time comes when this foetal or infantile development ceases to be upward, and is so directed as to answer to the life-wants of the particular species, so that henceforth and through life there is chiefly a development of lower characters, a slow movement towards degeneration

PHYSICAL STRUCTURE OF THE FEMALE

and senility, although a movement that is absolutely necessary to ensure the preservation and stability of the individual and the species. We might say that the foetal evolution which takes place sheltered from the world is in an abstractly upward direction, but that after birth all further development is merely a concrete adaptation to the environment.'

The infant type, i.e. the type towards which human development strives, is in all conditions relatively much nearer approached in the woman than in the man. Hans Friedenthal once emphasized the point that the 'infant' forms in woman exhibit in many respects what the most perfect forms of future mankind will be like, when he used Schiller's lines from *Würde der Frauen* (Dignity of Women) : ' Aus der bezaubernden Anmut der Züge Leuchtet der Menschheit Vollendung und Wiege ' (And the fascinating simplicity of the features portrays the perfection and cradle of mankind).

Ellis' view is undoubtedly right. Man and woman develop in the child (which to the end of the third foetal month is of common sex) in a mutually supplementary combination towards the higher type of human being. Nature repeats an experiment again and again, and though it may err here and there in regard to an individual about to enter the world, in the course of centuries it marches slowly forward and the higher development of the human being is eventually advanced.

It is merely a question of the point of view from which the matter is observed as to whether we consider woman as a kind of semi-human being or one that has progressed to a higher organization.

In any case (and here we turn back to the beginning of our speculations) man and woman are two distinctly different forms of the human species. Darwin has referred to the differences in the two sexes—which within certain limits are common to all races, and which were (as we may judge from the bones and skeletons which have been discovered) clearly pronounced even in the primitive Neanderthal people—as products of natural sex selection, and he sees in them part of the utility selection which is made imperative by the division of labour, that is, the particular tasks of the two sexes.

That the secondary sex characters, in fact, stand in intimate relation to the functions of the reproductive organs, and in particular to the generative glands (testicles and ovaries), is revealed by the effects of incidental disease, and certain experimental interferences (castration). On the other hand, however, the importance of the relation is overrated when endeavour is made to trace the whole of the female traits back to the functioning of the reproductive glands, as Rudolf Virchow, the celebrated German anthropologist, suggested is the case, when he ungallantly said that the female is only a female through possession of her generative glands. All the peculiarities of the woman's body and soul, according to him, or of her physical and nervous system, the tenderness and the roundness of her limbs which result from the peculiar formation of the pelvis, the development of the breast which is affected by the arrested growth of the vocal organs, that beautiful adornment, the hair of her head, and the scarcely perceptible down of the rest of her body, and also her depth of feeling, perception, meekness, devotion and faithfulness—in short, all those characters that we regard as most womanly and admirable in true woman, are but the outcome or product of the generative glands.

In outward appearance the proportions of the female figure differ considerably from those of man. In the woman everything appears softer, fuller, rounder, and therefore more graceful. This is due to the extra connective tissue and adipose deposits which are formed at the expense of muscle, and is also an outward expression of the graceful and more delicate skeleton. In general, where in man muscle masses bulk largely in the process of raising and lowering parts of the body, and where the bone surfaces are characteristically flat and angular, and there are osseous projections, there is in woman a rounder and more graceful system. In this way her figure acquires, from an aesthetic point of view, something pliant and submissive; her whole being takes on a tenderer attitude, while the soft rounding of the breast, trunk and hips seems to express repose.

This is in distinct opposition to the upstanding, self-conscious, even slightly flexed, attitude of the man's body, which, as Ellis says, seems instinctively to demand action.

While the female is much fuller in the buttocks, her trunk is comparatively longer and her limbs comparatively shorter than man's. The extra length of trunk is really brought about by the longer abdomen which has its explanation in the natural maternal mission of the woman. It is significant that in classic art, whether it be the statues of the Greeks and Romans, or the paintings of the old Italians and Netherlanders, one observes that a fuller, rounder abdomen appears

PHYSICAL STRUCTURE OF THE FEMALE 13

as one of the characteristic 'beauties' of the female.

Woman's limbs are not only shorter than man's, but they also differ in their separate parts. Amongst civilized races, at least, it is common for the woman to have a remarkably long index finger; and Pfitzner, whom we have to thank for a thorough investigation of the subject, conjectures that this was brought about by the continual use of the index finger in gesticulation, especially as, according to Weissenberg, this peculiarity is generally found amongst Jewesses. The nether limbs reveal a distinctive massiveness and shortness of the thighs, this condition being perhaps accentuated in appearance by the greater width of the pelvis. Together with this essentially different form in comparison with man, the lower limbs are not straight, but incline inwards above the knee, with a tendency to turn outwards below the knee, so that you have unmistakable X-legs, or, as in popular language, knock-knees (Fig. 2). It is the same, but in a lesser degree, with the arms: from the elbow the lower arm inclines slightly outward, though this is not so conspicuous in Europeans as in Japanese, and in the Oceanic peoples and negresses, who squat and support themselves on the arms, the resulting strain on the fore-arm over a long period having had effect on its shape.

The natural knock-knees of the woman are, aesthetically, the greatest blemish in the figure of the small, 'narrow-shouldered, wide-hipped, and short-legged sex', as Schopenhauer once somewhat vindictively, though correctly, said of woman.

Sculptors and painters, realizing this artistic fault, have frequently given their female models masculine hips and limbs, which is especially the case with Tintoretto (The Fall, Venus), and the school of Fontainebleau.

This physiological peculiarity is the cause of the somewhat comical figure cut by most women when running: the lower leg and the foot describing a highly ungracious straddling arc.

It is generally understood that the female body is smaller and lighter than that of the male: the difference in height in adults averaging about four to five inches (5 ft. 3 in.–5 ft. 7½ in.) and the difference in weight about twenty pounds (121 lb.–143 lb.). These differences are apparent at birth, though, of course, less distinctly, and quickly become more and more pronounced during the first years. But shortly before the age of puberty, a distinct change sets in, and for several years the girl

FIG. 2.—SHILLUK GIRL, UPPER NILE, WITH TYPICAL KNOCK-KNEES

PHYSICAL STRUCTURE OF THE FEMALE

remains larger and heavier than the boy of equal age. By about his fifteenth year, however, the boy begins again to forge ahead, overtaking the advantage held by the girl, and attaining his full height at about the age of 23 years. The girl practically ceases to grow with her twentieth year.

The form of the pelvis is a secondary sex character, so conspicuous and constant, that Darwin inclined to regard it as a sex character of the first grade. The female pelvis is most highly developed amongst Europeans: 'A small-hipped female figure is ugly, while the fate of the future generation is dependent on the essential development of the pelvis,' said Eckstein, the famous gynaecologist, and the Italian anthropologist Mantegazza, taking the same standpoint, declared, 'Without a wide pelvis, with rounded voluptuous hips, woman cannot nourish for nine months the fruit of her body.'

From time to time the female world has, for the sake of fashion and appearance, endeavoured to accentuate or reduce this particular development by all sorts of artificial contrivances, such as hip-belts, corsets, etc. But it is sufficient to say here that the female pelvis (Fig. 3 left) is, conformably with the special mission of woman, considerably broader, flatter and more roomy than that of man, whose narrow, small, and more upright pelvis is more reminiscent of the condition of the anthropoid apes and animals generally. The difference is so obvious that we can, for

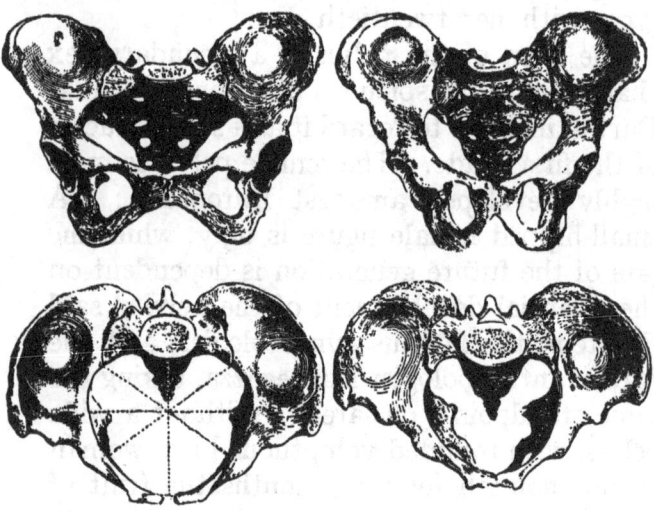

FIG. 3.—SEX DIFFERENCE IN THE FORMATION OF THE PELVIS.
Above: female (left), male (right), frontal view. Below: the same seen from above.

example, when a skeleton is unearthed during excavation, safely determine whether it is that of a man or woman by the form and build of the pelvis.

The female pelvis is distinguished outwardly by its fine and roomy construction, which in the sacral region is of a regular lozenge shaped, flat or slightly arched field, whose lateral limitations show dimples. The less prudish ancients who, in the classic cultivation of the female form of their time were well aware of these dimples, likened them to cheek dimples and ' Gelasimoi ' (smile dimples), while in many instances, in poems, etc., they were regarded and especially praised as beauty marks.

As has already been pointed out, the width of the pelvis and the particular construction of the female thighs and posterior parts go together. Our thigh-bone, as is well known, has a lateral neck growing out from the hip, and the globular head (or condyle) on this neck fits into a socket in the pelvis, thus linking it to the thigh. This neck makes an obtuse angle with the shaft of the thigh in the male, but is set practically at a right angle in the female. Here is again a typical secondary sex character which enables us to diagnose sex, man or woman, with absolute certainty, and it has been a factor of great value in certain kinds of investigation. The right-angled neck naturally tends to shorten the thigh of the female in proportion to the whole leg, and at the same time to broaden the ' tender fullness of the hips ', as the Minnesänger put it, in praising this peculiarity as an ideal form of beauty. The old Indian poets also praised 'heavy, mighty hips', and from statues such as the famous 'Aphrodite Kallipygos' (i.e. with the beautiful buttocks) we know how highly the ancient Greeks prized the broad hips of woman.

The Bible tells us that woman was made from the rib of man. As a result thereof man should be a rib short. But as a matter of fact the thorax of man is just about one rib depth (about $\frac{2}{3}$ in. to 1 in.) longer than that of woman. This perhaps explains the shortness of the female larynx with the resulting higher pitch of voice. Less roomy than that of man, the female thorax is like a cylinder and in transverse section appears almost circular; the male thorax, on the contrary, resembles the blunt end of a skittle at the top and is of oval form in transverse section. With European women it is found that the thorax has been considerably changed, or deformed, by the corset or stiff bodice (Fig. 4). Seeking the origin of these artificial aids to figure, one has to go right back to the days of degenerate Rome in the time of the Caesars. The really fashionable lady of those days bound up her bosom in a bandage in order to attain to the slender form of youth. From these comparatively harmless 'Strophium',

PHYSICAL STRUCTURE OF THE FEMALE

Mamillare of the Roman ladies, were evolved the stays which in the zenith of their fashion, towards the end of the eighteenth century, produced the 'wasp-waist'. About a hundred years earlier it was a Spanish mode to reduce the bosom, and the breasts were pressed down by lead tablets until, instead of prominences, there were actually indentations. Similar 'beautifying' apparatus in the form of plate-shaped pieces of wood are even to-day in use by the Dachau peasant women, and the maids of the Bregenz forests; women of German Tyrol, also, still wear wooden breast shields.

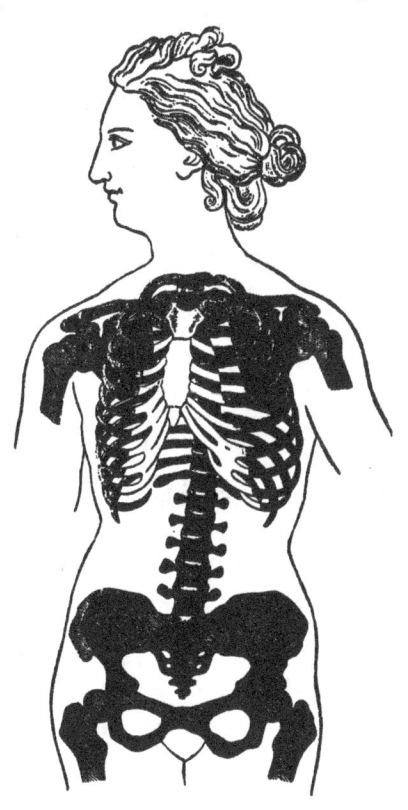

FIG. 4 (*a*).—THE EFFECT OF THE CORSET.
The Medici Venus with skeleton sketched in (according to Sömmering).

The practice of deforming the thorax is not restricted to European women : amongst some of the peoples of the Caucasus, for example, the Ossetes and the Tscherkess, the chest of the young girl is sewn up in a tightly-drawn leather sheath, in which she must remain till her wedding day. These artificial figure-forming aids, corsets, girdles and so on, have actually changed the European woman's system of breathing. She has become a chest-breather, while the man (and also the woman of primitive races) is a natural abdominal breather, that is, the respiratory method is that

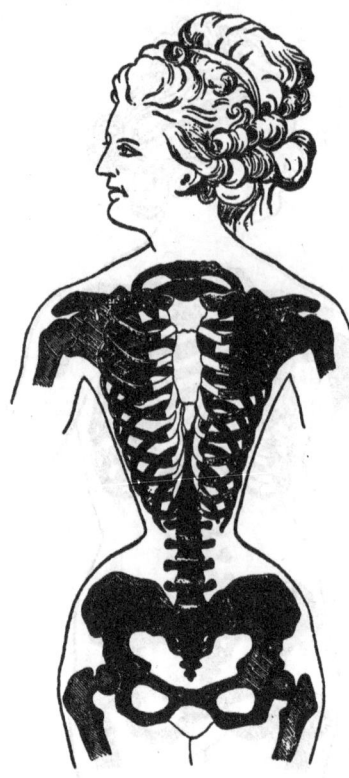

FIG. 4 (b).—THE EFFECT OF THE CORSET.

Fashionable lady of the eighteenth century, with skeleton sketched in (according to Rüdinger).

in which the diaphragm plays the chief rôle.

The British physiologist, L. Robinson, says with reason: 'I think it very likely one of the reasons (and there must be strong ones) for the persistent habit of tightening up the belly girth among Christian damsels, is that such constriction renders the breathing thoracic, and so advertises the alluring bosom by keeping it in constant and manifest movement. The heaving of a sub-clavicular sigh is likely to cause more sensation than the heaving of an epigastric or umbilical sigh.'

The vertebral column in woman, of which the twelve thoracic vertebræ form part, shows a remarkable singularity at the formation of the sacrum with the pelvis. It is well known that the last visible remains of the former tail, the coccyx, is made up of a row of diminutive, stunted vertebræ, which in unborn children still shows a considerable upward curve. Now, while the man has five remaining tail vertebræ, the woman has only four, a peculiarity which one would place on the credit side of the higher-development account were it not that the Asiatic anthropoid apes (Orang and Gibbon) have but three such tail vertebræ! It has been demonstrated that the spinal column of the human being is in process of shortening: and here apparently the female is in the van of the movement.

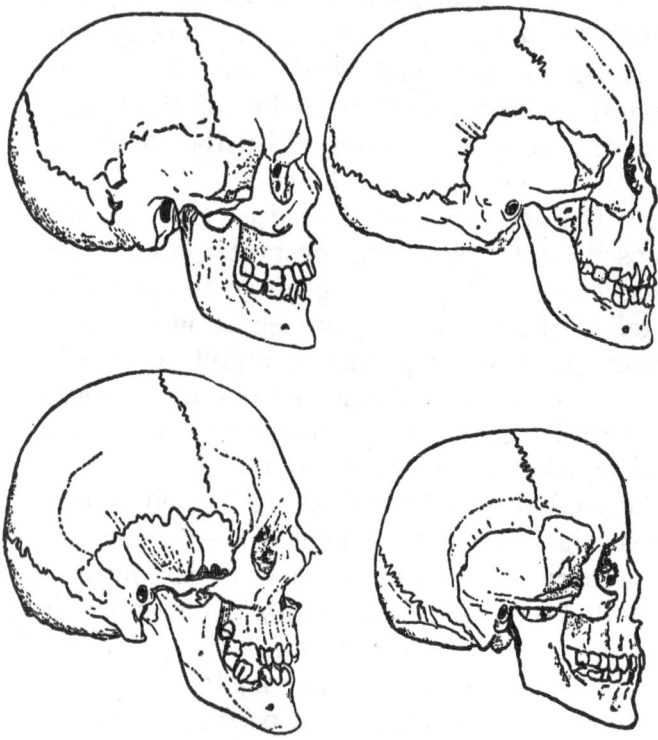

FIG. 5.—SEX DIFFERENCE IN THE SKULL:
Top row: male skull (left), and female (right), taken from a medieval Frankish grave.
Lower row: male skull (left), and female (right), from the present-day people of the Black Forest (Baden).

More important are the sex differences revealed in the skull (Fig. 5), the form and size of which bear comparison to the differences in the pelvis. If the various peculiarities are checked separately it will be found that there is not a single constant characteristic which is not decisive as to sex. Bring all the characteristics together and again no doubt can exist: an experienced observer will, in most cases, be able to decide the sex of the subject quite correctly. In general the cranial structure of the woman is less removed from that of the child, and in size, the skull of the European woman does not reveal a great advance from that of the so-called lower races. From these facts, various investigators have rashly decided that woman stands in a transition stage in relation to the more advanced human form. Indeed, one who poses as a grim woman-hater, a modern German author (Max Funke: *Are Women Human?*) would have one believe that woman, with a comparatively small cranial capacity, must be considered as a sort of ' missing link ', midway between man and the anthropoid ape, and should be labelled ' semi-human '.

Of the various sex differences it is remarkable that the female skull is on the whole smaller and, partly on account of the thinner bone, lighter than the male's. It is smoother rounder and generally more tender and fragile. As with the bony prominences of the face and body, so too the woman's skull is less strongly constructed than man's; indeed, some of these prominences are merely indicated in her. Especially is this true, for example, of the superciliary arch which is more or less strongly marked in the man, and is regarded by Ellis as a mark of ' distinctly retrograde character ' In primitive man (Neanderthal) and anthropoid apes, this arch is strongly in evidence. The absence of these over-shadowing ridges gives the eyes of woman a freer outlook, and her gaze therefore appears more open. The usual disproportionate forehead and parietal eminence of the infant remain, to some degree, permanent in the female, while in man they are modified and levelled out. The female forehead mounts straight up and turns in an abrupt angle to the sloped crown. The high arched skull top of the man, however, retreats gently. 'This straight-up brow', Ecker, the anatomist, considers, 'bestows decided nobleness to the female head.' Similar relations exist between the crown and the occiput: the male skull has an extensive vault, whereas the female's falls somewhat suddenly away.

The difference in the construction of the facial bones is very distinct. As with the cranium, so the face of the woman is decidedly smaller than the man's, in whom the lower parts—the jaws especially—are much more powerfully developed. The female jaw, for instance, weighs only 75 per cent. of that of the male, and, further, while the arc of the upper jaw in the latter is finely rounded, in the female it inclines to pointedness. A remarkable peculiarity to which Schaaffhausen drew attention reveals itself in the teeth of woman, and which C. H. Stratz considered a mark of feminine beauty: the top middle incisors in woman are especially broad, and this factor imparts a distinctive stamp to the features. Associated with this is a tendency for the teeth to slant outwards from the normal, and such prognathism is particularly typical in the lower races (Australian aborigines, negroes), primitive man (Neanderthal), and the anthropoid apes.

The capacity of the female brain-case corresponds to its lesser dimensions. According to R. Martin, the average cranial capacity of the normal male European is roughly 1,450 c.c., while for the woman it is only about 1,300 c.c. The lower the standing of the race, the less notable is this sex difference, which, with civilized people, becomes more and more distinct with physical growth and the more distinctive development of the sexual forms. Consequently, it must be considered as a particular secondary sex character.

The lesser capacity of the female cranium naturally makes for a smaller brain. The brain of the female European weighs on an average 120 gm. less than that of the male, and the difference is even appreciable in the newborn child, the brain of the female infant being practically 50 gm. less than that of the male. Many careful observers have postulated a close relationship between brain weight and intelligence. As George Buschan puts it : ' A larger, heavier brain must be regarded as a criterion of higher spiritual potence.' The figures given bear witness to the disadvantage of the woman in this regard, and the lack is endorsed on comparative tests of the form and finer construction of the brain. Anatomical details we can deal with later. It will be sufficient here to mention that these important differences in the construction of the brain (Fig. 6) are, without doubt, already established in the embryo, and that quite different typical laws of formation apply in regard to the convolutions of the brain of the two sexes. Though research in this delicate area is nothing like concluded as yet, we have to admit, with Max Bartels, a well-informed and impartial judge, that the differences which

PHYSICAL STRUCTURE OF THE FEMALE 27

have so far been revealed are important and characteristic enough to drive even the most zealous champion of woman's emancipation out of the field. In face of these facts it is but attempting the defence of a lost cause to take the stand with Ellis that ' A large brain is a perilous possession, and—so far at least

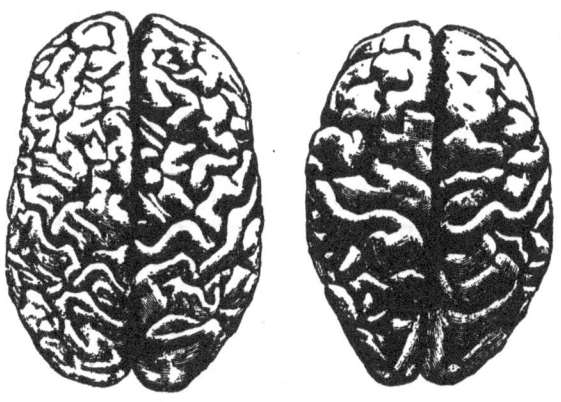

FIG. 6.—SEX DIFFERENCE SHOWN IN THE BRAIN OF NEW-BORN CHILDREN (according to Rüdinger).
Boy (left), girl (right). Above: forehead section. Below: the occiputal section

as this evidence goes—it is even more likely to be a perilous possession in woman than in man. A large brain is often inert or disordered, and fails to receive the rich blood-supply it demands ; there is much to be said in favour of a small, well-ordered, and active brain. It is possible that great thinkers generally have large brains, but among distinguished men of action a small brain seems to be quite as often found as a large one.'

The musculature of the female body lags far behind. In man the total muscle weight averages about 54 lb., that of woman only 32½ lb. Or, expressed in another way, the total muscle of the full-grown female is not a third of the total weight of the body (121 lb.), while the muscles of man (143 lb.) weigh more than a third. In particular the muscular development of back, chest and arms is weak in the European woman, though the muscles of the legs are pretty well equal in both sexes. In the circumference of the thigh we have the only feature where woman exceeds man absolutely. And this to my mind is due, certainly in part, to the peculiar formation of the female hips and buttocks.

The muscles of woman have a larger water-content than man's (74·4 : 72·5 per cent.), and this explains the softness of the fleshy parts of the female body. It cannot be doubted that a sex difference is here revealed, brought about as the result of different exercise. Among primitive folk, where the woman has to put her hand to heavy work, and generally works harder than the man, the arm and back muscles are better developed than in the case of the European woman. According to an account by the Italian Fiaschi of the battle of Adaua (1896), negro soldiers who had been crippled by the Abyssinians hacking off their feet, were carried for many miles from the field of battle on the backs of their women—certainly an exceptional feat of strength. Nevertheless, Waldeyer, the celebrated German anatomist, has asserted quite rightly that ' The organization of the male body is exactly what is required for speed and strength, and generally is, in this relation, far superior to that of the woman. This, furthermore, could not be altered even by change in the upbringing of the female and greater attention to her physical exercise '.

The stronger development of the muscles which is sometimes shown after prolonged, special exercise, does not (fortunately, I would add) rob the so-trained female body of its full and graceful roundness, which is peculiar to it as opposed to the male form.

Even the bodies of female athletes show (according to Schultze) a softer, more rounded outline, and not at all the rugged contour of the muscular man. This is due, of course, primarily to the greater development of fatty deposits in woman. These adipose cushions (subcutaneous fatty tissue) are located principally at the nape, over the shoulders, on the chest, where they produce the twin mounts of the breast, on the buttocks, and the fleshy parts of the limbs. The typical, normal distribution of these deposits over the female body we find attractive and beautiful—meagreness in woman may easily create an unpleasant impression. Men of our period may, from an aesthetic point of view, experience repulsion from over-fatness, but the old Netherlanders (one has only to remember the female forms of a Rubens) apparently loved the voluptuous, full female figure, while the South Italians especially prized the 'bella grossa' (the plump beauty), and certain Oriental people, Arabs, Egyptians, East Indians, various Negro races, the Hawaiians and Tahiti Islanders cultivate fatness in their womenfolk by regularly cramming them with fat-forming foodstuffs. 'The Oriental will pay a high price for the soft and pulpy,' says Mephistopheles in Goethe's *Faust*. One of the principal parts showing great fat development in the female is on the buttocks, and Martin, the German anthropologist, believes that to some degree a secondary sex character may be perceived here, 'which perhaps has come about by sexual selection'. To me also, there appears no doubt that erotic moments have induced such 'steatopygy'. Even in

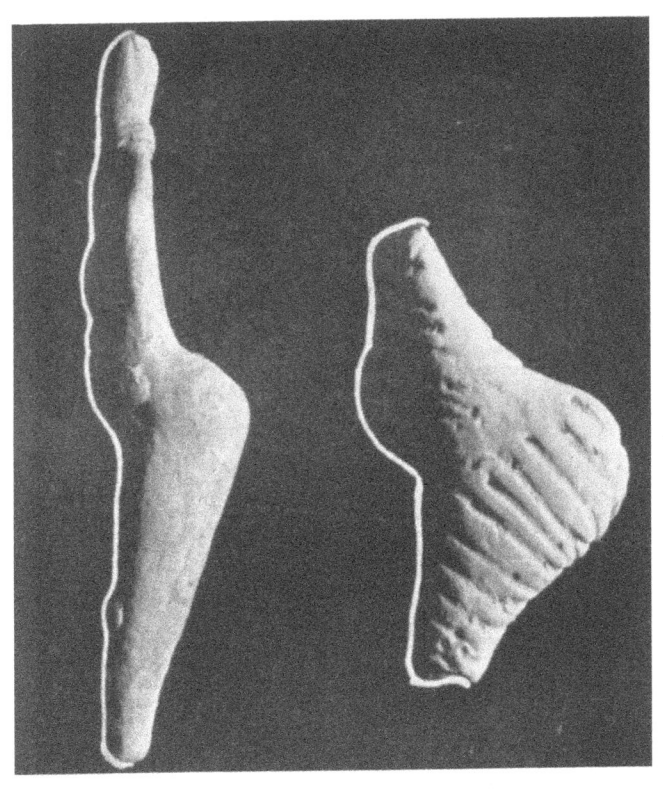

FIG. 9.—CLAY FEMALE FIGURE (NEOLITHIC) FROM CUCUTENI, RUMANIA, SHOWING STEATOPYGY

PHYSICAL STRUCTURE OF THE FEMALE 31

certain female statues from the early Stone Period to the end of the Diluvian, such as the so-called Venus of Brassempouy, Mas d'Azil and Laussel (South France), Mentone (Fig. 7), the Venus of Willendorf—Lower Austria—(Fig. 8), the female statues in clay from

FIG. 7.—FEMALE FIGURE SHOWING STEATOPYGY, CARVED IN STEATITE.
Aurignacian: Mentone cave.

FIG. 8.—THE WILLENDORF VENUS: LIMESTONE STATUETTE.
Aurignacian. From Willendorf, Lower Austria.

Cucuteni, Rumania (Fig. 9), of the Latter Stone Age, and so on, one notes depicted the great accumulation of fat in the sub-gluteal region. In the old Egyptian and pre-Mycenaean sculpture similar development may be observed. Amongst the races of to-day, these fatty accumulations are especially demonstrated in the South African Bushmen and Hottentots (Fig. 10). Cuvier once measured a Hottentot woman with such a protuberance which projected $6\frac{1}{2}$ inches from the base.

I would call to mind the popularity in the Rococco period, and then again about 1881, of the 'Cul de Paris', or bustle, which found favour with the fashionable world merely because the poet Jean Paul, like Albrecht v. Haller, maintained it gave a different appearance from the apes. May I also suggest that such 'form improvers' had no other object than the suggestion of steatopygy. For the rest, the particular development of these fat cushions, according to gynaecologists, has unmistakably some connexion with the generative glands, and puberty, confinement and especially the change of life, can be identified as causal periods. The tendency to plumpness and obesity is greatest during the critical years between forty and fifty.

While pigmentation and hairy covering play an important part as secondary sex characters in the animal world, where conspicuous skin colourings and richer hair growth are common to the male, in human beings sex differences in these directions are only important by way of comparison. The pigmentation of the

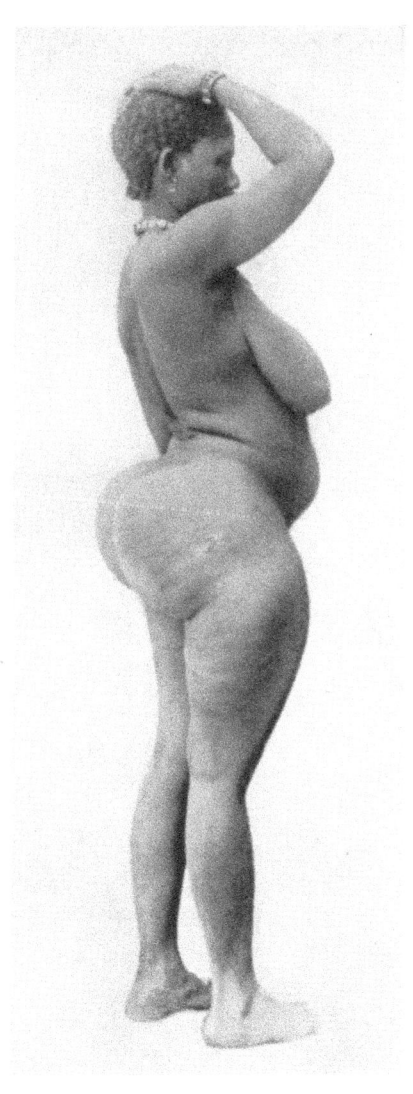

FIG. 10.—HOTTENTOT WOMAN WITH EXAGGERATED STEATOPYGY

female skin appears to be lighter in tone than that of the male of the same race, and further the newborn of coloured races are considerably lighter in colour than the adults, and only attain their full colouring after months or years. A somewhat more striking sex difference is noticeable in the hair. The foetal 'lanugo', that embryo-down thickly covering the whole body, being for the most part disposed of several weeks before birth, the permanent hair covering appears in two different forms: as infant, or secondary hair, and as adult, or terminal hair. This secondary hair differs only insignificantly from the lanugo-hair, and reveals itself in the head-hair, the eyebrows and eyelashes most distinctly, but it also covers the whole body as a fine down. This downy covering is far more strongly developed in woman than in man. What Hans Friedenthal, the accomplished German anthropologist, has to say as to the importance of this down in woman appears significant to my mind. It is well known that the roots of the hair are connected with special nerve endings, which make the hair exceptionally sensitive to touch: one can even go so far as to speak of a particular 'hair-contact sense'. The fine down which clothes the woman's body, therefore, results in an extreme delicacy of the sense of touch, which again, we know, is intimately related to sexual feeling. That this delicate contact-sensibility, as Friedenthal has it, plays a great rôle in the awakening of the maternal instinct, is certain; and in order to stimulate it the downy hairiness of the mother is not less important than that of the child. ' No other mammal possesses such general and delicate sensory organs for the reception of touch sensations as does the human being in its fine down-covered skin. As the man is so much superior in various characteristics to the beast, so the down-covered woman and the child, in regard to the finer sense of touch, are superior to the man with his rich terminal hair. And the sex-feeling, thus much more finely perceived by the woman, is of great importance in the service of race preservation. If the woman of the white races were to shake off her childlike characteristics through the exercise of masculine activities, and acquire, as she would perhaps, the male form of hair, a most important loss of maternal instinct would undoubtedly be unavoidable.'

In man the terminal hair begins to sprout at maturity, and, in both sexes as a matter of fact, it makes its first appearance in the armpits and the lower part of the trunk, then, in the male particularly, on the face as beard, and also on the chest and back. This growth is more or less thick, according to race. In the woman, moreover, it is generally restricted to the two first mentioned parts. Sometimes, and then only rarely, a growth of beard appears on the female, and this generally at a mature age, particularly at the change of life. This is chiefly seen in brunettes and Southerners, French and Polish women and Jewesses, and it gives a somewhat peculiar 'piquant' expression to the features. Buckman's observations, in which Brandt co-operated, suggest that the possibility of the development of hirsute facial growth on woman must not be excluded, indeed its ' appearance in the woman is probable '. Friedenthal also, basing his judgment on various observations, holds that ' it is very probable that the masculine activities now indulged in by woman will bring about the acquisition of a feminine beard '. In the study of the history of civilization, it is interesting to note the different aesthetic valuations at various periods of the terminal hair growth of woman. The Greek and Roman women shaved it off, and this is one reason why it is not shown in classic art, while the Mohammedan women are compelled by religious law to remove it. But the reports of the Seigneur de Brantôme tell us that the fashionable dames at the Court of Charles IX (sixteenth century) paid great attention to terminal hair, even as was done during the reign of his successor, by dressing and decorating it with ribbons and such like in the same way as the hair of the head !

A comparison of the inner organs of both sexes—ignoring the generative organs proper —shows only such differences as may be expected from the different sizes of the body and of functional capacities. This applies to a certain extent also to the larynx which, up to the age of puberty, has practically the same form and size, but then begins to grow increasingly in the male : the cartilage becomes harder, and forms, through the two angular fore-plates, the particular masculine ' Adam's-apple ' of the vernacular. In the female, on the contrary, the larynx remains more or less in its childish stage of development at about one-quarter to a third smaller than the male larynx, while, viewed in transverse section, it is rounder. In conformity with this the female vocal chords are considerably shorter (12–18 mm.), and the important difference in the vocal range of the two sexes is the natural result. The female voice is similar to the child's, only the timbre, as the musician says, is very different in the mature woman : it is more expressive, as one may clearly distinguish in choral singing. It is alleged that with the lower races the masculine larynx does not show such advanced development as the European's, and that the voice is not very different from that of the female in range. How close a relation really exists between development of the larynx, the pitch of the voice and the generative glands, we learn primarily from the custom of castration once practised by the Roman Catholics of Italy on boys intended for the church choirs, though we have still much to learn on this subject.

In this connection there are other glands of internal secretion to be considered, which seem also to have an important influence on the appearance of secondary sex characters, though the why and wherefore are still to-day an unsolved puzzle. Here we need only refer to the rôle in the production of goitre and cretinism played by the thyroid gland, which lies on the ventral side of the larynx. This, in females, is regularly larger than in the male, and, as the ancients were fully aware (Democrit, Catull), ' reflects all changes in the organism of the woman ', and as the anatomist Meckel once remarked is a 'repetition of the womb at the throat'.

A very remarkable sex difference, and one which in its fundamental importance is not generally assessed at full value, is in the blood. Our blood, as we all know, consists for the greater part of the blood fluid 'plasma', and the corpuscles (red and white) which float in the fluid, or to put it more correctly are 'suspended in the plasma'. The blood has the very important function, on the one hand, of carrying to all parts of our system the material necessary for the life processes of, and, on the other hand, of eliminating and passing out waste matter useless to the organs, the products of metabolism. The red corpuscles have also the particular function of adjusting the gas exchange, that is of extracting the oxygen from the air drawn into the lungs, and delivering it to the various organs, a task which they are enabled to perform by reason of their haemoglobin content. The blood of the adult woman by comparison is richer in plasma and in water-content (80 : 75 per cent.) and produces far less red corpuscles (in one cubic millimetre of blood, 4·8 : 5·3 million), and thereby the haemoglobin content is less (13 : 14 per cent.). It seems that this sex difference becomes especially marked at puberty. This gulf between the sexes cannot be bridged and no further evidence is required to show how extraordinarily important the blood is in the whole life-process.

If we glance at the comparative anatomy of man and woman, we shall be prepared to subscribe to Ellis's words that 'a man is a man even to his thumb, and a woman is a woman down to her little toes'. But we have seen that the various differences according to their kind, and in their particular importance, are not all to be assessed in the same way, and are not all equally valuable. If we desire to form a sound judgement on the position of woman in nature and in social life, we must first attempt to answer the question as to which differences have been brought about by nature, and which are the outcome of civilization. In a new hypothesis set out by the erudite Freiburg anthropologist, Eugen Fischer, it is considered that a large number of the peculiarities of the human sexes which are claimed to be racial differences, are really domestic characters, or, otherwise expressed, domestic animal attributes, as Darwin, in a letter to A. R. Wallace, March 1867, already hinted at. Fischer brings forward an imposing mass of arguments in support of his view that 'all characters which are met with in man as racial differences appear also in domestic animals as such, and vice versa, most domestic animal peculiarities are again found in man as racial idiosyncrasies '. In the same way that man during thousands and thousands of years has directly influenced the physical and mental being of domestic animals, by regulation of their nourishment according to his will, and by directing the course of their propagation, so has he, further, proceeding along the same lines and with parallel results, built up and developed individual racial peculiarities from his own stock type. This applies in particular to the style of the hair, pigmentation of the skin, size and proportions of body, and so on.

This extremely fascinating hypothesis is illustrated by an inspection and critical review of the secondary sex characters of the human being. Fischer himself regards ' steatopygy ' as a typical domestic animal character, finding parallels in the haunches of certain breeds of sheep and the heavy shoulders of certain oxen. One may, therefore, consider the fat deposits on the hips and thighs of European women as features of domestication. In my opinion, and I have expressed it before, there can be little doubt that erotic factors have had their influence and effect. The cultivation of the

PHYSICAL STRUCTURE OF THE FEMALE 41

female bosom may be regarded from the same point of view. The ' permanent breast ' is, as Friedenthal says, a pronounced domestic animal peculiarity, for it does not appear in any wild forms of life. Upon reflection this will not seem so strange and unimportant when we realize that on the lowest rungs of civilization's ladder, the female is regarded as a special kind of useful domestic animal and commonly treated as such. Of particular interest, in this regard, is the reply that a companion of Darwin received from a native of Tierra del Fuego. Asked why in times of famine the dogs were not killed by preference instead of the women, he laconically replied, ' Hounds can catch otters, old women cannot.',

The slighter muscular development of the European women is traceable to civilized conditions, for in general it is solely through the practice of dancing, where there has been early training, that muscular power approaching that of the male is met with. During the course of an evening's dancing our ladies cover a good many miles, at any rate a distance which they would perhaps be reluctant to march along the open road. I must, however, admit that the activities encouraged by modern sport have undoubtedly improved things in this respect. Amongst many primitive people the women are as strong as the men. In proof of this Bancroft cites the characteristic reasoning of a North America Indian chieftain: 'Women are made for labour. One of them can carry or haul as much as two men can do.' What may be achieved through physical exercise by European women is shown by the examples of the female workers of Lancashire, and the women who during the war accomplished heavy tasks in the munition factories.

Gynaecologists have observed another aspect of the subject, and have noted that a great development of the voluntary muscular system reacts unfavourably on the involuntary muscles (womb, bladder and other organs), which are of great importance in women. G. J. Engelman, the American gynaecologist, comes to the conclusion as a result of his observations amongst English and American gymnastic teachers, circus artists, and such like, that 'excessive development of the muscular system is certainly unfavourable to maternity, for it would seem to be a fact that women who exercise all their muscles excessively meet with increased difficulties in parturition'. The advantage which thousands of years of exercise has given to man cannot be surpassed in a day and night.

A concomitant of civilization, a domestic peculiarity, or a product of sexual selection, just as one cares to express it, is seen in the decidedly smaller skull of the woman, in its lesser capacity and in the lighter brain weight with all the consequences thereof. A continued special demand results in an increased flow of blood to an organ, which in turn stimulates energetic growth with corresponding increase of its specific constituent parts. So our brain reacts to the stimulus of strenuous mental activity. All cultural advance demands this increase of effort. Buschan demonstrates this for us very clearly in his interesting study *Brain and Culture*. Those people who are ranked low in the civilized scale possess a much lighter brain and a smaller cranial capacity than modern highly developed races. The mental worker again stands out above the average.

A comparison of French skulls of the early Stone Age with some of the twelfth and of the nineteenth century shows the increase of brain-case capacity in conformity with cultural advance. But, on the other hand, E. Schmidt, dealing with skulls of Egyptians of the past two thousand years, and Sergi, comparing skulls of the inhabitants of Imperial Rome with those of the modern Piedmontese, have been able to demonstrate that, with the decline of spiritual culture, an undeniable decrease of cranial capacity could be observed. In accordance with this rule we might expect that the average of European women would stand much above that of peoples of lower civilization. This is indeed true, for they are vastly superior in this respect to the Bushmen, Australian natives, Papuans and Weddas. In similar ratio the highest measures that have been found in the capacity of skulls of European women are just as high or even higher than the middle measure of men's skulls of the same race. In other words, the smaller skull capacity and lesser brain weight in woman, conformable to her mental inferiority, are to a certain degree domestic peculiarities.

This undeniable ' minus ' of to-day—and we have already remarked that the sex difference seems generally less the lower a people stands culturally—may possibly be eliminated within certain bounds, through properly directed mental training. Yet it must be borne in mind in this connexion that the advantage which man has gained through thousands of years-long exercise can only be very gradually overtaken. Here again we must put a note of interrogation: Similar differences, that is of the brain development of the two sexes, are to be found in our nearest animal relatives, the anthropoid apes. Indeed, we find this important factor in all the higher animals, so that cultivated breeding alone does not explain it.

With the difference in the male and female pelvis it is otherwise. The particular form of wide and roomy pelvis in the European female is to a degree a cultivated product, as is shown by its gradual development amongst the highest races, and this development has kept pace, more or less, with the constantly increasing size of the skull. In the lower races it is not so marked. Here the narrow, less roomy female pelvis (compare Fig. 11 and Fig. 2 with Fig. 3) approaches in shape the small, steeper form of the male, and, therefore, of the anthropoid apes. However, the fundamental differences are attendant upon the natural mission of the woman, i.e. Maternity. ' When the Greek Sculptors ', says the French anatomist Topinard, with justice, referring to certain female statues of post-classic antiquity, ' gave woman a narrow pelvis, they not only robbed her of one of her most appreciated features, but degraded her to an animal form.' Nature and culture lie here in constant opposition to one another : civilization produces larger head measurements in the children

46 THE OPPOSITE SEXES

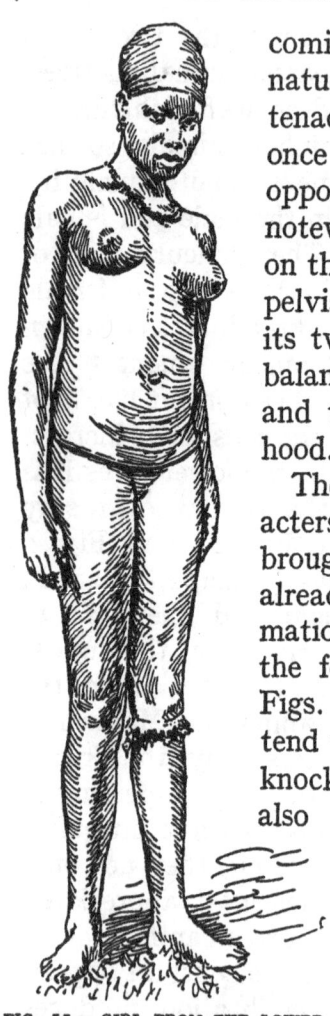

FIG. 11.—GIRL FROM THE LOWER NIGER, WITH TYPICAL SMALL HIPS AND CORRESPONDINGLY SMALL, NARROW PELVIS.

coming into the world; nature contrariwise holds tenaciously to certain sizes once attained, and this opposition is shown in the noteworthy compromise on the form of the female pelvis, which conforms to its two main tasks: the balancing of the trunk and the duty of motherhood.

The typical pelvic characters of the woman are brought about, as we have already seen, by the formation of the top joints of the female thigh (see also Figs. 2 and 11) which also tend to the production of knock-knees. They are also brought about by other natural causes to a certain extent, and instead of correcting them, civilization has, on the contrary, a tendency to exaggerate them.

The composition of the blood too is another natural condition, and it appears to me, as I have already said, a factor of the utmost significance in our attempts to arrive at some decision on the subject we are discussing. The extraordinary importance of the blood for the animal organisms and their various functions leads one to suppose that the 'minus' revealed in the composition of the female blood—a constitutional defect, as one might say—must be a mighty hindrance to progress toward higher power in brain, musculature, and indeed in every organ in the formation of which the male is more favoured. It is not so much the fact that, given equal conditions, the woman generally has less blood than man—that is conclusive, or that her lung capacity is inferior, as that in each cubic millimetre of blood she lacks a round half-million of red corpuscles, and, as a result, the percentage of haemoglobin which means so much in the functioning of the organs is considerably less. This natural physiological inferiority, which the lower mammals also share, prevails invariably, and it is not easy to conceive how the difference can be made up. In view of this indisputable distinction between the sexes, it is questionable if the female can, through bodily development, ever fully attain to the cultural heights which male organism has reached. At any rate the change cannot take place over-night. For the development and raising of a lowly characteristic to a higher standard, great periods of time, and a long lane of generations, biology teaches us are necessary ; and so the female of to-morrow will still be the female of to-day, and woman of the conceivable future will not differ considerably from her present-day representative.

In spite of all this, there exists the possibility of a great advance, and we ought to-day to lend a hand in the attempt to raise woman to a higher plane. In this province the efforts made towards the emancipation of woman are fully justified in so far as they respect those limits set by nature. All undue hastening of the rate of progress will be bitterly avenged, however, for as the great Swedish naturalist Linnæus once remarked, ' Natura non facit saltum '.

CHAPTER II

THE SOUL OF WOMAN

"WOMAN has no soul and no ego. It is external appearances that make up the ego of the woman. With the female thought is a hurry and a scurry, a superficial sipping of many things to which man, who goes down deep into matters, scarcely gives any attention. She tastes and nibbles and gropes around without a grasp of main factors. And so, the mental activity of woman being a kind of tasting, taste in its widest sense, is the most distinctive feminine quality, the chief attainment a woman can reach and one which she can bring to a certain state of perfection.'

This is the description in the modern philosophy by Weininger of the mental and spiritual abilities of woman. This too is, speaking generally, the opinion of Schopenhauer, Eduard von Hartmann, and Nietzsche, modified only by the individual temperament, and point of view of each. Indeed, Nietzsche, in his self-conscious intolerance, went so far as to regard those who held a different opinion as 'typical shallow-pates, shallow in instinct, and generally suspect'. The creator of the Superman added that such persons 'will probably be superficial in all fundamental questions, and never get down to the depth of things'.

Nearly the same idea is found in Bernard Shaw's philosophical comedy, *Man and Superman*, and also in that ironical letter which he wrote about the same subject to Arthur Bingham Walkley: 'Sexually, Woman is Nature's contrivance for perpetuating its highest achievement. Sexually, Man is Woman's contrivance for fulfilling Nature's behest in the most economical way.'

Modern philosophers and critics of woman have called in to their support a number of doctors who, being professed psychologists, are naturally qualified to judge; men such as Ferrero, Lombroso, von Krafft-Ebing, and perhaps the psychologist Möbius, whose polemic 'On the physiological weak-mindedness of the female' created an extraordinary and not unwarranted sensation.

Möbius would imply, in using the rather exaggerated expression, 'physiological weak-mindedness', that there is a mental and spiritual inferiority in woman as compared with man, somewhat as a child may be considered weak-witted by comparison with adults, and in the same manner as a decrease of mental ability becomes visible—earlier or later—with growing age. 'Just as man and woman have similar cerebral convolutions, only with different features,' Möbius goes on to say, 'so both have similar spiritual properties. No acquisition is apparent in one sex exclusively; a plus or minus alone forms the difference. . . . One of the most important differences is that instinct with woman plays a greater rôle than with man. One may speak of a series which begins with those beings acting instinctively only, and ends with those whose actions are the result of excogitation. It is characteristic in mental development that instinct gradually subsides, thought and consideration displacing it more and more. We understand by instinct the performance of an appropriate action without the person realizing why; as soon as a certain circumstance recurs, some apparatus within us is set in motion and we carry out the necessary action as if driven by an external power. It is a matter also of instinctive discernment when we effect an unconscious or automatic decision. Fundamentally, no action or perception takes place without instinct, for a part of the process always falls within the unconscious field; but there are differences of degree. The greater the part played by the individual consciousness in perception and action, the higher grade of the individual development, and the more independent is the individual. A middle course between mere instinct and clear consciousness we call feeling. To do anything from feeling, to be guided by feeling alone to a judgement of truth, is to act half instinctively. Instinct has the great advantage of being reliable, and it gives no trouble; feeling carries but half this advantage. It is her instinct that makes woman similar to the animal, makes her dependent, yet sure and serene. Herein lies the true power which is her wonder and attractiveness. Very many of the female peculiarities are related to this animal similarity.'

Möbius ascribes want of judgement and lack of creative imagination on the one hand, and absence of independent thought on the other, to these peculiarities: ' Women are morally narrow-minded or defective, their feeling makes them unjust.' Further, he speaks of their incapability of self-control, their emotional vehemence, and dissimulation.

THE SOUL OF WOMAN 53

He closes by saying: 'After all the weak-mindedness of the female (which is a natural, primitive characteristic) not merely exists but is a necessity'; and he demands: 'Protect the woman against intellectualism.'

Allan, the anthropologist, declares it paradoxical to maintain (with Madame de Staël) that there are no sexual differences in mentality, and that those of intellect are but a result of education. A woman with a masculine intellect, he says, is as great an abnormality as a woman with a male breast, a male pelvis, or a beard. Parallel with differences in the physical organization of the two sexes, there exist radical, natural and permanent differences in the mental and psychical configuration of man and woman.

The gynaecologist, Max Runge, emphasizing the physical differences which 'Nature has produced, unalterably, between the two sexes', arrives at a similar decision. He asserts that 'the woman is in no way equal to the man, but possesses absolutely different qualifications'.

Even though it may be taken for granted that these matters have been correctly observed and truly valued, yet these investigators have overlooked one important cause of different peculiarities: here again the above-mentioned hypothesis of Prof. Fischer as to the domestic animal qualities of the human race (see p. 40), when applied to the relations of the two sexes, proves to be extraordinarily productive in the effort to attain to a correct judgement. Much more must be said on this subject later on. Here it is only necessary to mention, as a parallel to the generally known facts, that the mental and (if one may say so) moral qualities of the domestic animals in comparison with those of their nearest wild relatives, must all be looked on as inferior. What philosophy, with its human observations and thoughts reaching back to primitive times, designates the mystic-religious conception ' soul ', or calls ' spirit ', is to the modern naturalist the accord of all bodily activities. The scientist perceives the brain as the organ of the soul, and certain parts of the so-called cerebral cortex as the seat of the mental activities. Special areas stand in undoubted relation to quite definite psychical actions. To distinguish between things of the world about us and those of which we are made conscious by perception, nature has given us the organs of sense, the functions of which are ordinarily called sight, hearing, smell, taste and feeling (tactile sensibility, sensibility to temperature, pain, and so

THE SOUL OF WOMAN 55

on). If we wish to judge correctly about any existing difference of the spiritual and intellectual peculiarities in man and woman, we must first examine how far the brain and sense organs of the woman differ from those of the man in construction, and especially in function.

In the first chapter of this book there are several references to the brain (see pp. 26 and 43). There exist, without doubt whatever, important differences between the male and female brain, differences of weight as well as of finer modelling—differences, moreover, which are prominently revealed at birth and even before. Rüdinger, the Munich anatomist, whom I follow here, emphasized the fact that in the newborn boy all three diameters of the brain (length, breadth and depth) are greater than in the girl. Up to the seventh and eighth foetal month, the convolutions of the female brain remain considerably more simple than in the male (see Fig. 6), so that the frontal lobe of the girl gives an impression of smoothness or simplicity. All secondary transverse fissures are already present in the male brain, while in the female they appear quite elementary and show a slower growth. The male parietal lobe is distinctly characteristic, and different from that of the female, for while the frontal and occipital lobes are still comparatively smooth, they soon show deep fissuring, and appear conspicuously different from their surroundings. The anatomist Huschke holds, rightly I think, that the parietal lobe is a favoured section of the brain in the male. In spite of many individual exceptions, Rüdinger comes to the conclusion that it is undeniable that different typical structural laws hold for the cerebral convolutions of the two sexes, and that these laws are in operation even before birth.

The Berlin anatomist, Waldeyer, who made especial investigations in regard to twins of different sex, found that the formation of the fissures were far better developed in the male than in the female child of the same parents.

Nevertheless, I am inclined to believe that these differences must be regarded in a certain measure as being caused by cultural conditions. The brain of the female may be trained, as I have previously stated (see p. 44), to the same development as the male's by suitable exercise, just as the brain of the European has been raised to a far superior standard than that of the Bushmen, Weddas, Australian aborigines, and such. But it must again be emphasized that this progress is only possible over long periods of time. Observation of too rapidly forced development of the brain amongst the North American negroes has shown that the lighter, less capable brain easily succumbs in the struggle for life. The number of mental defectives amongst these negroes has risen by fits and starts to an extraordinary height since liberation from slavery, while before this time the negro slaves showed a much lower percentage of insanity than their white masters.

The fact that amongst people of modern culture insanity has increased conspicuously, and claims its victims especially amongst the females—as Ellis says, ' an unduly heavy tax which women pay for the privilege of taking part in our modern civilization '—should for us, also, in this connexion, be an effective ' Mene Tekel '.

Comparative tests of the organs of sense of both sexes, and, further, the keenness of the sensitive faculties, are as yet but little cultivated. Results of exact research, as G. Heymans, the Groningen psychologist, justly complains, are hopelessly contradictory as a rule, and conform but imperfectly with the results of former observers.

One notes in the eyes of man a wider space between the pupil centres, which is greater still among primitive, hunting people than Europeans, and must be of value as regards better sight. Here I must mention, by the way, that the human suckling only acquires control of the parallel motion of the visual axis after many months of effort. In general, the average visual faculty of males is better than that of females, even as with primitive peoples it is considerably greater than that of Europeans. Darwin attributes this inferiority in Europeans to the aggregate and inherited effect of decreased use through numerous generations, and one would surely not err in tracing the comparatively sharper sight of the male to his original hunting and warlike activities during thousands of years.

Carter, the British oculist, found that minor defects of sight in woman were much more common than in man, and considers it due to their weaker muscles, which are less able, as a rule, than those of man, to maintain the strain of prolonged efforts of accommodation (focussing of varying distances), or of convergence (adjustment to the visual line in the distance). In this relation Ellis observes that imperfect accommodation might well be regarded as a domestic animal peculiarity. The comparison of the eyes of wild animals with those born in captivity support this conclusion.

The fact that, on one hand, colour sensitiveness in man is of a much wider range and keener than in woman appears singular, but, on the other hand, colour-blindness in man is about ten times as frequent as in woman. This puzzling circumstance is further complicated by the observation that colour-blindness among primitive folk is very rare, while among civilized races it is found to a far greater extent in those classes whose social conditions are unfavourable, and in the intellectually lower strata of society.

We are still less informed about the differences in the sense of hearing in man and woman. One observer finds greater keenness of hearing in man—another in woman; at any rate, according to Galton's tests, the man seems to have greater keenness in his sensitiveness to pitch.

The sense of smell has in mankind generally sunk to a secondary level. It is much better developed among the primitive races than among Europeans, and, according to Bailey and Nichols, it is 'much more delicate' in man than in woman. The relative keenness of smell in child, woman, and man is set out in the following proportion 5 : 70 : 900. It has further been found by experiment that an odour is detected by a woman somewhat more slowly than by a man. But the opinions of some critics to the effect that woman frequently uses (as she already did in Ancient Egypt) perfumes of oppressive strength because of her lack of olfactory sensibility, is hardly tenable. Such use of perfume is employed partly to cover the unpleasant odour of perspiration, and partly as an erotic, though inefficient allurement. Ellis reminds us that St. Clement of Alexandria (d. A.D. 220) wrote a ' delightful manual ', *The Paedagogus*, for use of his semi-pagan ' Christians ', in which the woman needing perfumery is given the advice that she should choose only such unguents as will not be overpowering to a husband.

The measurement of the sensibility of taste is quite impossible. In ordinary daily life, as Zwaademaker remarks, it is associated with, and is scarcely separable from, sensations of smell, touch and temperature. In general we are only able to discern four qualities of taste—sweet, sour, bitter and salt. From the researches of many observers we learn that in woman the sense of taste is more delicately developed for all qualities except the salt. This seems also to apply to primitive people. We must consider that acuteness of the senses, in their relations and differences, has to be acquired, and that exercise, without doubt, develops and sharpens it. Furthermore, heredity plays an important rôle in this. I am therefore inclined to believe that the remarkable difference in the sensibility to taste in the two sexes is derived from the following fact: Originally, amongst the primitive races, and for many thousands of years up to the present day, the male alone consumed animal food—game—and so acquired the greater sensibility to salt food, while the female had to be satisfied with fruit and other sweet, sour and bitter tasting vegetables (see p. 90).

Among the perceptions of the skin, the sense of touch and contact is, according to evolutionary teaching, the oldest and most primitive. Sensibility to pressure and contact is found even in the most elementary animalcules. It is better developed in woman than in man, finer in the townswoman than in the peasant woman, and it may be perfected by exercise. As to the difference in sensibility to temperature, research up to now has not enabled us to draw definite conclusions. But numerous observations have been made in regard to the sense of pain, which, while not proving lesser sensibility to pain in woman, at any rate reveal a remarkable indifference to hurt. This ability to bear pain better than man, associated with a greater power to endure injuries and overcome them, seems to be a primitive legacy. Woman, in this regard, is similar to primitive people and to the child. On the other hand, it may be, as Ellis conjectures, that the thousands of years of woman's subordination to man have played a part, and that submissive tolerance of pain is an inherited peculiarity. At all events well-known surgeons, Billroth and Eiselsberg, for example, affirm the existence of the condition, and every dentist has the opportunity to observe it daily.

If we recapitulate all we can ascertain on the subject of the difference of the sexes in regard to their psychic organs, these being, in a certain measure, the primary source of all mental activity, we find the woman undoubtedly lacking in relation to the principal senses (sight, hearing and smell), and above all in the central organ, the brain. Only in the development of the sense of taste and touch is woman the superior of man. Yet such superiority does not predicate a higher development but rather the persistence of a deeper, more primitive degree of evolution. In this case it is not easy to give a precise and conclusive answer to the question as to how far these differences are brought about by culture and how far by nature. In regard to the brain, I have already pointed out that in all higher developed animals, especially in the anthropoid apes, distinct natural differences in the size of the brain of the two sexes may be found to exist (see p. 26). Therefore, the difference in the size and development of the brain (fissure modelling) of male and female may not in all probability be solely traceable to cultural breeding. Be this as it may, woman does tackle mental work with less efficient organs than man. This fact alone explains why she lags behind in psychical ability. This is undoubtedly true of the highest abilities, for there is no woman who can approximately attain the degree of perfection that man reaches mentally and psychically. Here and there, certainly, and in every age, some woman exceeds the average of man in ability; for example, Caroline Herschel (1750–1848), the famous sister of a still more famous brother, and Elizabeth Brown, the astronomers; Sophie Germain (1776–1831) and Sonia Kowalewska (1853–1891), the mathematicians; in physics, Marie Curie, the able working comrade of her husband; poetesses like Sappho (about 610 B.C.), Annette von Droste (1797–1848), and

Selma Lagerlöf; painters like Rosa Bonheur (1822–1899), and in our days, Kaethe Kollwitz (b. 1867). Yet all these highest elevations of feminine intelligence and psychic talent remain far below the summit of man's attainments and potentialities in the same sphere. It is most remarkable, perhaps, that even in music there has been no creative female genius (no composer at all worth mentioning), and Rubinstein once remarked in wonder: 'The two particularly natural feelings of woman —love for man and tenderness to the child— have found no expression in music by any member of the female sex! I do not know of a single love duet, or lullaby, composed by a woman which has attained to classical importance.' Mantegazza mentions that in a biographical dictionary he only found from 4 to 8 per cent. of female names, and, according to Bourdet, out of 54,000 names of French inventors who had registered patents, only six were females. As against this August Bebel, in *The Woman and Socialism*, enumerates a series taken from an American technical journal of important inventions which were the work of women, and he submits that amongst the problems elucidated there are many which ingenious men have vainly attempted to solve. This may be correct, and as an addition to Bebel's list of Technical Inventions, we might mention the most satisfactory invention ever made and evolved by woman—the earthen cooking pot (see p. 93).

This does not prove anything as to the innate psychic equality of the two sexes. To arrive at a true judgement, one must not, as Heymans rightly warns us, compare the highly gifted woman with the average man, but the talented woman with the talented man, or the average woman with the average man. It will then be shown that no woman has ever created anything equal to the creations of the most ingenious man. It is more remarkable, yet really decisive, that against the great number of exceptional men in every sphere, only a very meagre number of women can be opposed. In order to satisfy oneself on this point, it is necessary only to take up the story of any science or art, bearing in mind that in most of these spheres man has never imposed restraint on woman. On the contrary, within certain circles and at certain periods, such as the epoch of chivalry and the Italian Renaissance (see p. 145), woman received most careful education and training in preference to man, and almost at all times poetry, music and painting have played a greater rôle in the education of the girl than of the boy. The cause of the difference in average capacity and highest accomplishments in the two sexes must be sought elsewhere than in the region of cultural development.

The results of numerous new observations in schools and universities in America, Great Britain, France, Germany and Holland bear this out. These show unmistakably that to-day 'superficial education and lack of knowledge are not the sole cause' of the intellectual inferiority of woman. The woman, according to these examinations,[1] is generally superior to the man in zeal, diligence, perseverance and patience, but she lags behind him in sagacity. The woman's interest lies in concrete realities, in that which can be touched and seen, not in the abstract, the ideal, the imaginary. Her 'intellect' shows —from a psychological point of view—not so much 'understanding' in the narrower sense of the word, or intellectual power, but 'intuition', the intuitive power, even 'divination', which I here would like to interpret by 'instinctive apprehension'.

---

[1] For details I must direct the reader to the valuable work of the Groningen psychologist G. Heymans, entitled *The Psychology of the Woman*. This author is very cautious in his judgement and I am indebted to his book for much information.

The woman allows herself to be guided by instinct far more readily than does the man (see p. 52), and so her logical process more frequently leads her to act in the 'unconscious' or subconscious sphere. Investigators agree remarkably, though they may differ in other respects, that the stronger emotionalism, greater excitability, irritability, impressionableness, excessive sensitiveness, the prevalence of sentimentality, and so to say, the inconsiderate response to every 'stimulus', mark an important psychic difference in woman.

The woman reacts to much slighter stimulations than does the man, and much more emotionally than he to equally strong stimulations. Emotionalism is a quality associated with primitive, subconscious mental activity. It is governed by nerve centres which phylogenetically are the oldest and in closest connexion with the involuntary circulatory and muscular organs, such as the heart, bladder and womb. A sensation affecting the nerve system must first stimulate the convulsive action of the heart, muscles and other organs, before it is reflected and eventually emerges in the brain as the effect of an emotional act.

It is not my intention to deal critically with all the psychical peculiarities (those related to stronger emotionality) of woman, but rather to pursue only the question as to which of the peculiarities and differences are the result of natural conditions and which may be regarded as the consequences of culture.

The results of research into the subject of heredity disclose many remarkable facts. They reveal to us that the psychical qualities which prevail in the son depend particularly on those of the father, and that those of the daughter are related to those of the mother. But they also teach us that in this relation we have to differentiate between specifically male and female psychic sex predispositions, as the son and the daughter may exhibit certain peculiarities which are absent in the father or mother. This applies particularly to emotionalism, which in all circumstances is stronger in woman than in man. Investigations into the subject of heredity show us further that the influence of inherited predispositions greatly exceeds that of education, and daily observation proves that this inherited disposition in the female is simply her inherent nature, which now and then strives to strip off the equalizing varnish of culture covering the richly-coloured picture of her real nature.

' Women are naturals, elementarily organized, and personifications of the elementary power,' the spirited German essayist, Bogumil Goltz, once observed, and in Heymans' view too the woman feels culture as a fetter and as a violence offered to her nature.

Disposition and inherited disposition, which we have put on the same scale, are, however, in no way one and the same thing. The long-continued effect of culture, that is to say of social conditions, is probably able to bring about a not unimportant alteration of the original, natural disposition. In fact, every development in nature depends on a transformation effected by changed conditions of living. The bodily and mental qualities of the domestic animals in comparison with those of their untamed relatives, disclose to us the positively revolutionary influence which culture may exercise.

It certainly gives us reason to think when we learn that the weight of brain of the domestic animals, compared with that of their wild relatives, has decreased considerably, and when we realize that the tamed animal, on relinquishing his psychic independence, mentally recedes far behind his wild progenitor. Perhaps many psychical peculiarities of the woman must thus be considered as ' domestic animal qualities ' (see p. 39) bred into woman from the earliest days of mankind. It may be imagined, for example, that the submissive character of woman, with its consequences—timidity, insincerity, dissimulation, and so on—belongs to such domestic animal qualities.

If we go to the root of the matter, however, we find that this submissiveness is in no way confined to the human female. It is also developed in the same degree in the higher animals, especially in the apes (see p. 87). Steinmetz rightly remarks, in regard to this problem, that the minor bodily power of the woman cannot be the sole reason for such submission. The physically weaker human being has never submitted to wild animals which are much stronger, and if the woman ' had originally been equally intelligent, equally strong in power of will, and equally egoistic as the man, she would scarcely have allowed herself to be subdued by the man '.

After all we cannot see how stronger emotionalism, which is generally recognized as the most marked pyschic quality of the female, can be a product of culture. It has its basis, as we know from experience, in those regions of the soul which are entirely outside the influence of our will power.

It may be conjectured, therefore, that

emotionalism might have been developed and intensified by 'natural selection', as the man consciously selected for propagation only those women as were naturally highly emotional.

According to psychologists, the following qualities are closely co-related to emotionalism : changing moods, timidity, irresolution, lack of courage, long-lasting effect of grief, rapid subsidence of anger, variability, frequent changes of sympathies, frequent laughing, limitation of consciousness, susceptibility to auto-suggestion, imagination, intuitive power but lack of comprehension, inclination to avoid the abstract, and above all intuitive thought, impulsiveness, inclination to fanaticism, manual skill, vanity, craving for power, strong compassionate feeling as well as extreme cruelty, tendency to exaggeration yet honesty and reliability, religious tendency, and frequency of psychic disturbances. 'It is plainly shown', says Heymans, who has cited these instances, ' by experience and can easily be made clear that all these qualities are connected with emotionalism. They will be most likely more characteristic of the woman than of the man as long as she remains particularly emotional, as she is and was in the past.'

Is it possible to believe that the wild man of the glacial period, the primitive people of to-day, or even the man of a higher sphere of civilization, would choose his mate, the bearer of his children, even to the slightest extent for qualities (which he might consider as of value to him), such as manual skill, honesty and reliability ? Does not the man of to-day, on the contrary (ignoring the fact that social conditions compel him oft-times to decide on a wife with regard to money and rank), choose his wife, for the most part, for wholly different reasons, and chiefly for quite external, physical attractions ? And when, in spite of this, in spite of a lack of intensifying natural selection, and the counteraction of the man in suppressing many qualities through education, female emotionalism has been preserved unaltered with all its correlations, must we not consider this emotionalism a fundamental quality of the female soul given by nature ?

It is so obvious that the greatest thinkers of all times have seen in this or that manifestation of emotionalism the most characteristic quality of the female ' psyche ', and people in their wisdom have at all times treated this characteristic in proverb.

Without doubt many of the psychic traits

arising from excessive emotionalism, which seem undesirable and even disgraceful in the woman of to-day, will be changed by systematic influence. Even the fundamental evil will, when it is clearly recognized, be cured to a certain degree, for the unconscious, and instinct, are after all not absolutely unalterable. But this cannot—as I have emphasized in regard to physical peculiarities—be brought about between sunset and sunrise, and certainly it will not be so simply accomplished as the little lady of to-day seems to fancy when by 'shingling' and the 'Eton crop' she would, with real feminine logic, disprove the truth of the old Turkish proverb 'Long hair—quick comprehension'.

CHAPTER III

THE DEVELOPMENT OF THE SOCIAL POSITION OF WOMAN

THE cultural history of mankind begins with the appearance of the man of the diluvian epoch, that is to say the man of the earlier glacial period, whom Klaatsch, with the privilege of the anatomist, comparing his entire physical properties, classifies, on the basis of structure and function, as ' Animal still among the animals '. With this stage begins for us the possibility of an insight into the social relations between man and woman. This first glimpse is very restricted, and the farther we press towards the beginning of the Palaeolithic Age, the more impenetrable becomes the fog which shrouds it from us. Various meagre skeleton remains, a few rude sculptures and carvings on bone or stone are all we have left to give us any information of the man and woman of those early times from which to draw conclusions. We must be very careful in our deductions, indeed, because the material which we have at hand to-day is too frail on which to base a sound judgement. One is not infrequently compelled to come to *a posteriori* conclusions, in the absence of one or other accustomed phenomenon allowing of a comparison with primitive folk of the present day.

It is strange, for instance, that of the diluvian skeletons excavated up to now the greater number are of males, while only very few of females have been found : the women had mostly been interred together with the men, as, for example, was the case at Oberkassel (not far from Bonn, in the Rhineland), and in the 'Grotte des Enfants' (Childs' Grotto) at Mentone. Should we therefore not conclude that the man of the glacial period did not rate woman particularly high, in that he only very rarely honoured her with a careful burial ? In cases where man and woman have been buried together, the conjecture must not be ignored that the woman had most likely been a kind of sacrifice offered to the man, or, rather, had been regarded as a chattel on which he laid a claim for service beyond the grave. In other words the woman was killed on the death of the man, and interred with him.

From numerous indications, which are not

to be misinterpreted, we know that the savage of the Ice Age had a naïve faith in immortality. To him, as it is with most primitive folk of the present day, death was (as Heinrich Ploss expresses it) 'not dying in our sense, but a journey from which there was no return'. His dead, whose ghosts he feared might haunt him, he tried to prevent returning by fettering the corpse or covering it with heavy stones. For the journey to the Beyond the traveller was furnished with all he had valued in life : adornments, stone weapons and tools, and also his servant—the woman.

When we recall that with the Germanni (and until a very short time ago with the Hindu—see Fig. 12) the widow was, originally, burnt together with her dead husband ; that once upon a time among the Thracians, according to the report of Herodotus, the favourite wife ' was killed over her husband's grave by his relatives and buried with him ', that not so long ago the South African Basutos clubbed the widow to death (as Joest records) at the husband's burial, and that in the Fiji Islands (South Seas) the woman was strangled and interred with her husband, our hypothesis may appear more probable than the supposition that the pair found in primitive graves

FIG. 12.—HINDOO WOMAN THROWING HERSELF ON THE FUNERAL PYRE OF HER HUSBAND

were simultaneously taken off by some epidemic illness.

Nothing so far tends to show that the wild man of the Ice Age looked upon his woman as anything more than a chattel, a possession that he might deal with according to his desires and could exchange or even kill at will. A systematic comparison of the oldest cultural epochs with the types of human beings among most primitive races of to-day justifies our view that the position of the woman was a most wretched one.

Almost all pictorial representations of the old Stone Age prove to us that woman was regarded by man as being essentially a means of satisfying his desires, and, characteristically enough, these representations begin in the Aurignacian period (about 40,000 years B.C.) with crude reproductions of female sex organs, in the form of stone sculptures such as recall to mind the rude drawings of street arabs of to-day. Somewhat later we find small female statues in which, with a single exception (the ivory head of Brassempouy, Landes, South France), the artists have utterly neglected the features, but exaggerated the sexual attributes. They are all of mature female forms, most unsightly according to our ideals, types, as I quite agree with

Hoernes, the Venetian historian, such as very likely were not only appreciated in life, but actually bred (see p. 30). Besides these female statuettes with startlingly emphasized sexual attributes, drawings and carvings have come down to us (chiefly in Předmost in Moravia—Fig. 13). Though I do not entirely agree with the opinion of the scholar of prehistoric times, Abbé Hugues Obermeyer, who focusses on a certain point, that all the above-mentioned female representations are 'idols', realistic, erotic symbols of productiveness, I am inclined to believe that the Předmost carver intended to represent the 'miracle of procreation', that wonder from which a later and more just appreciation of woman was partially to emerge.

It is scarcely credible that mankind came to realize the causative connexion of pairing off and conception at a relatively late date only. We must, however, remember that the long period between conception and birth made such realization very difficult for the Stone Age man, especially as he did not possess domestic animals in which the comparatively short duration of gestation would enable the observer to grasp the connexion.

Even to-day there are primitive folk who know nothing about this natural process. The Australian aborigine, for example, be-

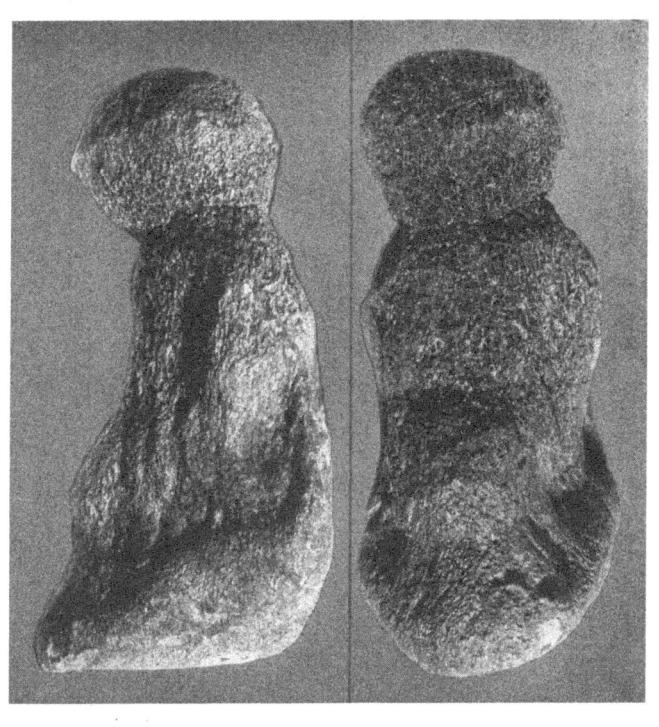

FIG. 13.—IDOL OF A PREGNANT WOMAN CUT IN MAMMOTH BONE.
AURIGNACIAN, PREDMOST

lieves that children are the result of tiny spirits, reborn ancestors, whose souls are personified in animal forms that force their way into the body of the mother-to-be at some given opportunity. Only when she feels the first movements of the child does the woman realize her condition. We find this unsophisticated belief in an unnatural, 'immaculate' conception, running through the mythology of numerous civilized peoples, and even in the Christian religion. The unmistakable physical connexion between mother and child (to take it literally) at birth, served to suggest, progressively, the first true conceptions of the real process, and repetition of observation led to further, more correct, ideas of the natural relations : this resulted in widespread matriarchal organizations in the primitive stage of civilization, of which more is said later.

On the lowest level of culture woman has been valued as a thing, a chattel or, as Klemm strikingly expresses it, as 'the prime domestic animal', by the man who procured her by robbery or purchase. She had only duties to perform and enjoyed no rights. The man then was 'The master', and the woman, as the African explorer, Franz Hutter, has described her as he found her among the pastoral tribes of the Cameroons, 'physically and socially of the lowest rank, whose chief task it is to do the work and bear children for the Lord of Creation'.

As with so many native people, the lot of the Australian aboriginal woman, as described by K. E. Jung, is not to be envied. Already at birth, maybe, she is promised to a great warrior, and she is handed over to him as soon as she reaches the necessary age of puberty, which is about her twelfth year. However she may, in girlish repugnance, struggle against marriage with a peevish, faded old man, there is no escape. Any resistance is overcome by beating, sometimes to the point of serious injury. The runaway from the hated yoke is punished by having her leg pierced by a wooden lance, so that a repetition of flight is impossible. The investigations of the excellent English ethnologist, W. E. Roth, show that the entrance of the maid into connubial relations is accompanied by extremes of sensual barbarity, in which the old men, as heads of the tribe, act the chief part. The younger man can only obtain possession of a woman with the greatest difficulty; though occasionally the older ones abandon their women to young members of the tribe. Entirely broken in spirit, the poor creature

THE SOCIAL POSITION OF WOMAN

submits to her hard lot, which is rendered still worse to the young woman, by the ill-treatment she has to suffer from her predecessors and associate wives whose place as favourite she perhaps takes. As to her tasks, she has to build the wattle and skin huts, she must gather wood for the night fires in front of the hut, she has to hunt up all kinds of small animals, and collect herbs, dig out roots with a sharpened billet, grind the gathered grain between flattened stones and from this flour make cakes which she bakes in the hot ashes of the fire.

In the meantime the man engages in hunting, but generally he reserves the prey for his own personal use, or, as Howitt reports, according to strictly observed communistic laws, shares his ' bag ' fairly with his hunting companions. Eyre saw men after long hours of fishing consume all they had caught, not saving a scrap for wives and families. Yet at about noon these same fellows hurried off to the settlement in order to get their share of the provisions which the women, as a rule, had brought home. When the tribe is wandering, the man will carry only a light spear, while all the family possessions are packed on the shoulders of his wives, who not infrequently carry four or five great bundles each.

In addition, there may be an infant who rides astride on the shoulders of the mother with its tiny hands holding fast in its parent's matted hair. Sometimes the little one is simply put into the skin bag which is formed by the cloak of fur worn by the mother.

In the nomad life which the Australian native, as a hunter, is forced to live, a crowd of tiny children would be a hindrance. Accordingly it used to be the custom to kill off the infants, and Jung states that this practice obtains even to-day in those districts which cannot be reached by the long arm of the white man's law. The murdered children were frequently eaten (according to the same authority). Cases have been reported of the custom of killing the new-born babe and placing a pair of dingo pups to be nursed at the mother's breasts, which shows how much more valuable in this low state of culture the possession of a dog appears to the native hunter than that of a child.

That the lower races, and not necessarily only the very lowest, are accustomed to rate their women just as domestic animals, a few further examples will show.

Of the Samoyeds (Ural territory) in the eighteenth century, the traveller Pallas reports that the women are even more unfortunate and worse treated than those of the Ostjaks. With these nomad tribes, the women have to do all the household work, and besides must build huts and dismantle them, pack and unpack the sledges, while at the same time slavishly serving their men in every way. The men, on the contrary, excepting for a few evenings of dalliance, scarcely take notice of or deign to throw a kind word to the women. Yet this is not all: the woman is regarded as an impure being. When she has constructed the hut, she must not enter it before she herself and everything which she has sat upon—the sledge and every article she has carried into the hut—has been fumigated over a fire of reindeer hair. If the woman intends to unbind the bundles of clothing and other goods from the sledge, she must not do it from above, but must crawl under the runners to which the reindeer are harnessed. In the hut, after all this procedure, a post is planted in the ground opposite the door to mark the boundary beyond which the woman is not allowed to pass.

The North American Prairie Indians speak of the women, says Catlin, as ' hewers of wood and carriers of water ', and the Sioux chiefs, whom the explorer had painted, scornfully requested him to destroy their portraits when they learned that he intended to paint pictures of women also.

In Catlin's opinion, the women of these hunting people are in no other relation to the men than 'menials and slaves'. At the age of ten to twelve years the maidens are already sold by the father without their wishes being at all consulted. The woman, in addition to manifold household duties, which include not only cooking, but also wood-chopping and water-carrying, the preparation and dressing of the buffalo and deer hides for tents and clothing, and skins for sale to the white man, must also till and cultivate the fields. It is she who erects and dismantles the wigwams, and, when moving, packs them together with the household goods on the horse-drawn sleds, and then, frequently with a large bundle of clothes and such-like on her back and perhaps a child at the breast, or in the cradle slung from her shoulders, marches at the horse's head very often for days. At night, if a halt is made, the woman must first prepare food for the family before she dare think of resting herself.

The women never eat together with the men; they are also denied participation in religious ceremonies, festivals and dances.

With most African tribes the woman is subjected as a slave to every whim of man; she is ' a utensil, or a beast of burden, to be replaced by another when she is worn out '. In buying her, Burton once said, speaking of the Wasaramo (East Africa), the man makes no more to-do than if he were trading for a goat. Should he wish to get rid of his wife, he merely hands her a straw as the symbol of his desire. If she does not then leave him willingly, she is driven away by force.

The lowly social status of African native women, however, is now so well recognized that it is scarcely necessary to emphasize their utter degradation further.

I should like, however, to record a few characteristic features in regard to customary greetings which reveal the servility of the African woman in a rather curious way. The women of the Batlakoa, in the North Transvaal (according to the missionary Wangemann), throw themselves at the feet of the chieftains ' in an attitude of worship and, with the fingers and hands laid together, make certain gestures suggesting veneration. Thereafter they crawl past the men in the same submissive attitude '. The celebrated German explorer Nachtigal gives a similar report on the women in Wadai (Central Sudan) and of the

Chozzam Arabs. 'It seems very remarkable to me that the women of these Arabs had to follow the customs of the Wadais and creep past a group of men, always keeping a proper distance. Dirt and rain was not sufficient to permit a relaxation of this. I saw beautiful young girls with silken loin-cloths making their way through mudholes on their knees. Even when the men invited them to assume an upright position the gentler sex seldom dared take advantage of the permission.'

There cannot be the slightest doubt, in view of available information, that the social position of the woman in the earliest days of civilization was similarly degrading. If we seek for the fundamental explanation of such absolute submission to the will of man, we find it—speaking generally—in our animal origin, especially in our relationship to the gregarious animal types. For many thousands of years the tribes of the human race were compelled to live under conditions similar to those of the animal herds, above whose level man had scarcely risen up to the glacial period. In animal herds, however, in accordance with that inexorable law of nature which by favouring the operation of selection leads to the improvement of the breed, only the right of the strongest in the struggle for food prevails, for they will be the best nourished, and be able to survive longest. The leader of the herd, generally the oldest male, claims, by virtue of his natural rank, absolute right over the females, and, as we can observe in all wild animal herds, the females submit instinctively to this law of nature, which promises them a degree of security and supply of food.

Observations by the zoologist Zenker furnish an impressive picture of the communal life of a troop of gorillas tracking through the forests. When out seeking food, the younger beasts are at the head of the troop; then follow the females, and the old animals bring up the rear. The leader moves slowly, and frequently raises himself to full height to look around and make sure nothing suspicious is within sight. If there is no danger in view he will, when hungry, sit down at the foot of a tree, while the females bring fruit which they lay at his feet. From time to time two of the females will nestle up to him and he will place his long arms round their shoulders, seeming to jest with them, judging by the snarling, screeching and squealing, and sometimes a sound which might be considered as laughter. If he scents danger, the leader drums softly on his cheeks with the flat palms of his hands, and then trumpets with wide-open jaws. This signal sets the troop in flight. Then as soon as the leader catches sight of the enemy, he begins to drum heavily with his fists on that tough, leathery, rumbling chest of his, and turns furiously on his adversary.

Another family scene was once witnessed by Hugo v. Koppenfels, the German sportsman. The females and cubs had to pluck fruit from the adjacent trees for the lazy family tyrant, and if one of them were not quick enough, or pulled down too much for herself, the male dealt her a hefty box on the ears, and grunted his abuse.

I would like to amplify these pictures of the family life of the anthropoid apes by reports of other observers. Jasper v. Oertsen states that every evening, during their migrations, the gorilla females build nests for themselves and their young to rest in during the night. Sometimes these are constructed on the ground and sometimes 10 to 18 feet high in the branches of a straight-trunked tree. He once found, in close company, sixteen such sleeping nests. The male gorilla, however, according to Koppenfels, passes the night curled up at the foot of one of the trees, in order to be ready to protect his troop against night attack by beasts of prey.

A critical time comes for the leader of a troop when, with advancing age, his strength begins to wane, and one of the younger males shows a desire to supplant him, or when there is a meeting with another male gorilla in the prime of life. There then takes place, as has been observed by Karl W. H. Koch, a very bitter fight, and the winner secures the booty; that is, the females and young pass into the possession and guardianship of the victor. The vanquished erstwhile leader withdraws resentfully, and, pursuing his lonely way, becomes a dangerous solitary ranger of the woods.

We may legitimately suppose that the life and customs of the original men-troops, those ' animals among animals ' as Klaatsch, the Breslau anthropologist, calls them (see Klaatsch-Heilborn, *The Evolution and Progress of Mankind*, translated by Joseph McCabe, London, 1923), were not very different from what has been described above; indeed, impartial consideration reveals in this description of social life amongst the gorillas, many remarkable parallels to the life of the more degraded native peoples of to-day.

In a very singular work, *Urkommunismus und Urreligion* (Primitive Communism and Religion), the sociologist, H. Eildermann, takes the view set out here, and endeavours by its help to establish the theory that conjugal life among the lowest hunter-men is, in the first instance, a business arrangement, which may be attributed to the various tasks allotted to the sexes in social housekeeping.

As the human being by the nature of his teeth and bodily organization depends on mixed fare, flesh and vegetable food for nourishment, there must have come about in very early times a separation of the sexes for the tasks of securing provender. The men sought meat by hunting, the women, together with the children and perhaps also the old men now hardly strong enough for the strenuous exertions of the hunt, gathered fruit and dug for roots, just as to-day we may see done amongst the Australian aborigines. At first perhaps the men consumed their booty alone, or shared it with the hunting company, eating the raw flesh without preparation, just where the beast was killed, and yet in camp they would claim their share of the vegetable food gathered by the women. There must gradually have come about an exchange of victuals between the sexes, though probably at first only by reason of an abundance of meat, which no one knew how to preserve, or from sexual impulses, and the stirrings of the common senses (pity—charity) which are distinctly pronounced in the herding animals. Man needed vegetable food also, and this he could most easily obtain through the woman. And so a change gradually took place in the relationship between man and woman, a change, scarcely noticeable at first, which was in favour of the woman. This change was much strengthened when it was discovered how to make fire and guard it safely.

How man discovered fire, how he learnt to 'tame' and maintain it, and how eventually he learnt to produce it at any time and anywhere, cannot be described here (I have dealt with the subject in my book *General Ethnology*, Vol. I, Leipzig, 1915). In regard to this I need only mention the extraordinary importance which fire had for primitive man besides its use for the preparation of nourishment.

Thanks to this 'safe watchman', says Julius Lippert, the well-known historian, it became possible for mankind to extend their area of diffusion, on the one hand, into all those tracts hitherto given over to the animals, and, on the other hand, into the cold north and rude mountain regions : and thus set in motion the mainsprings of the history of mankind.

The savage of the Ice Age found in fire, for one thing, a protection against the cold, and also against the night attacks of the gigantic beasts of those days. He also utilized it for the roasting of the meat he had obtained hunting, as is proved by the many discoveries of carbonized bones among remains of Neanderthal times (about 150,000 B.C.).

The maintenance and care of the fire was, in the earliest days, one of the tasks allotted to the female, because the man could not, while out following the chase, carry with him this sensitive and dangerous element which was so difficult to transport. Care of the fire, Lippert says further, henceforth formed the centre of those domains which woman controlled. This made the household more difficult to move from place to place, but it added to it an attractive power of a more permanent kind; for, previously, woman's physical allurements alone, and then only intermittently, had exercised any fascination over the male.

The man, who formerly had sought the company of the woman only at limited periods, now became a regular guest at her hearth, and was more than ever dependent on her. The flesh food of the man was made more savoury and digestible by being roasted over the fire, and the hope of enjoying this brought him back to the household with his prey.

THE SOCIAL POSITION OF WOMAN 93

As a result woman now attained a position in which she might demand a share for the benefit of her household. This provided grounds for a contract involving mutual duties, and this contract very considerably improved the social position of the woman.

There was something primitively reminiscent of the earliest days of civilization in the symbolic preservation of the tribal fires of Vesta by the virgins in Ancient Rome.

Later, with the discovery of how to produce fire at will, man tended once more to become a wanderer. But he was hardly able to reconquer his once unrestricted sovereignty after the woman had made her most ingenious discovery: that of the earthen cooking pot. This invention, with all its world-wide consequences, to which belong not only the considerable improvement in diet, but also the ' James Watt tea-kettle ', and subsequently the steam engine, remains even up to this day the greatest thing woman has ever achieved. From it dates the commencement of the subjugation, or voluntary subduing of the man ; in the early days of civilization at least the somewhat sarcastic proverb which says that man is governed through his stomach was more or less justified.

In manifold ways woman extended the

range of her particular activities later on. She has developed and monopolized important trades and professions, thus considerably expanding her sphere of influence. There can

FIG. 14 (a).—AGRICULTURAL DIGGING STICK USED BY THE PRESENT-DAY HOTTENTOTS.

scarcely be any doubt that observation during the gathering of fruit and digging of roots led to the realization of the possibility of regular crops, and consequently by natural steps to a primitive husbandry, which facilitated the task of procuring vegetable foodstuffs. Up to this day the simple style of garden cultivation with spade and hoe (in their original form, one a pointed billet and the other a bent bough) is with primitive races nearly everywhere the work of the woman (see Figs. 14 *a* and *b*). The ethnologist Weule says: 'A final example of this primeval division of work is even found to-day in the care of the garden and its urban substitute, the balcony, which still remains

in the hands of the lady of the house.'

It is hardly possible to decide with the same degree of certainty whether plaiting, spinning and weaving have also been feminine

THE SOCIAL POSITION OF WOMAN 95

activities from the beginning. But one can imagine so, because such handicraft, owing to the lack of wool-bearing domestic animals, must originally have been carried out with the raw material of plant growths. In the

FIG. 14 (b).— NUPE-NEGRESS AT WORK IN THE FIELD WITH A HOE.

Swiss lake-dwellings (Neolithic—about 5000 B.C.) many textures of flax, but only few of wool, have been found. Amongst primitive peoples of the present day both men and women, here and there, engage in plaiting and weaving (Fig. 15 *a* and *b*), so that generally, in the province of handicraft, the conditions obtaining among primitive races afford no satisfactory grounds for comparison, for the original boundaries of the divisions of labour have usually been obliterated. The men, for various reasons, have usurped female occupations, and burdened the women, on the other

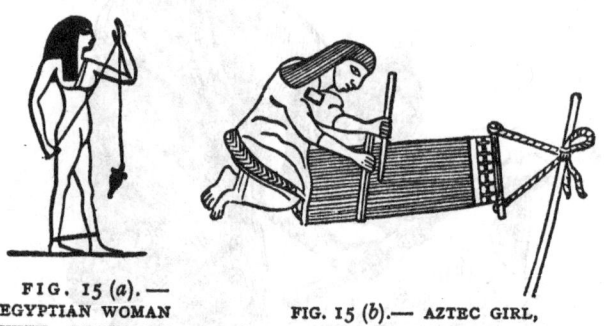

FIG. 15 (*a*).— EGYPTIAN WOMAN WITH SPINDLE SPINNING WHEEL.

FIG. 15 (*b*).— AZTEC GIRL, WEAVING.

hand, with the more degrading work, including especially masculine manual labour. Not rarely, remarks Heinrich Schurtz, the historian, in regard to such matters, one finds in this the starting-point of that later contempt for certain handicrafts, which has only after a long fight been overcome by advancing culture. The ignoble position of the weaver and the potter until the end of the Middle Ages in Germany must have sprung from the fact that these handworkers were engaged in what originally was a feminine occupation, for no other reason for derision can be found.

The subject takes a more comical turn with the tailors, who, while avoiding mistrust of their profession, have for hundreds of years been the butt of general jest and scoffing on account of their supposed effeminate nature and weak physique.

The status of woman as compared with that of man experienced a considerable improvement when primitive man had gained a better understanding of the connexion between procreation and birth (compare p. 79). This knowledge—arising to a certain extent from observation of certain periodical sexual functions of the mature woman, gestation, and birth—led to the custom known to sociologists as 'Matriarchate'. Owing to the practice in primitive times of the 'collective marriage' of all men and women within the tribe, and the uncontrolled promiscuity, to which no doubt we have authentic parallels in the relations of most of the other higher mammals (which is to be accepted as the original condition of sexual relations between human male and female), the establishment of fatherhood in individual cases was as good as excluded. But as against this there must have been observed, in every case, the literal blood-relationship of the mother and child. The nourishment of the infant, and its helplessness, caused a long-standing close connexion of the two ; for the emptying of the milk glands was a physical necessity for the mother. This seems the place to advert to the fact that among most backward races of to-day, mothers nurse their offspring much longer than is customary with civilized people. The average period is about two to three years. The Australian native mother suckles her child for six years ; the North American Indian mother up to the twelfth year, and the Eskimo (King William's Land), it is said authentically, up to the fifteenth year. Of course, economic conditions may play an important rôle here, and just for this reason I am persuaded that among the primitive people of the Ice Age there was also of necessity a longer period of suckling.

Out of this natural, intimate connexion of mother and child arose the strong spiritual stirring of mother-love, which we find pronounced in the higher animal world, rising even to self-sacrifice, a sentiment, however, reciprocated with similar devotion only by human children.

Mother and child established in this way an exclusive association ('Clan', 'Gens') to

THE SOCIAL POSITION OF WOMAN

which the father was a stranger, and not blood-related; in which, at any rate, he had not equal membership.[1] To the woman this association brought a valuable enrichment of her power, in that the grown-up son's feelings, arising out of the sense of the natural relationship, were those of the natural supporter, while the daughters became helpers in all that was particularly female work.

In favour of the validity of this view we find not only that the matriarchal system, with its manifold consequences, is in being among many lowly races of the present day (Australia, Africa, America, and Asia), but that the idea of the matriarchate was undoubtedly prominent in and among cultured peoples in ancient times as far as the position of the woman was concerned.

Amongst the records handed down to us dealing with the cultural epoch of Babylon—though to be sure it applies but little to our subject—we find that in reference to mother and father, the woman and the man, the mother and woman are invariably mentioned first.

[1] It would take us too far beyond the range of this study if I were to deal fully with the historical development of matrimony. I can only indicate isolated phases of the continually changing connexion between man and woman with which to illustrate certain of my arguments.

This clearly indicates a reminiscence of mother-right in a civilized era where the pre-eminent social position of the man was in all respects unshakably established. Further, the high position held by the woman in old Babylon is documented by equality of rights in religion and at the bar of justice, as we may learn from certain statements. We read, for example, in the time of King Hammurapi (about 2250 B.C.) of women who had their seats in the Temple, and we find the names of women as witnesses in legal documents and such-like.

More exact information is available in regard to the position of the women in Ancient Egypt. Nothing shows more distinctly the original power of the conception of mother-right than the fact that on various monuments of private persons (statues, sarcophagi, tomb-walls), in the biography of the parentage of those persons treated, there appears continually the declaration ' son of such and such mother ', or ' begat of such and such mother ' ; the name of the father being rarely given.

Again, at the time of the Greek conquest the Egyptian bore only the mother's name ; then quite gradually this usage came to an end and the father's name was acknowledged as the proper one. Already in the oldest hieroglyphic writings the woman is described as 'neb-t-em pa', that is 'mistress of the house', or 'neb-tur pa' which is 'great mistress of the house'. Similarly she was occasionally called by her husband ' dear mistress ' or ' mistress of the house beloved by your husband'. Taking this point of view of matriarchy, the reports, so long rejected by Egyptologists (such as, for example, the German poet and historian Georg Ebers), of Herodotus, who about the middle of the fifth century B.C. travelled throughout Egypt, become intelligible and credible.

Among the Egyptians 'the women go to market and bargain, the men on the contrary stay at home and weave', this learned Greek historian and keen observer tells us. ' The sons are not obliged to support their indigent parents if they do not wish; on the contrary, this is the daughter's duty.'

Four hundred years later Diodorus confirmed this and stated the fact that the woman held a splendid position in the house, adding that the Queen in Egypt possessed more authority than the King. Diodorus mentions also that in the marriage contract the man vowed obedience to his future wife. The testament of a distinguished Egyptian of the name of Sekieh which has been found lately discloses to us the fact that the

Egyptian woman controlled her own fortune, and could dispose of it as she liked; further, the aged testator left his property to his brother, i.e. his nearest living 'blood relative' according to the old conception.

Such notions fostered also, 'as a most natural arrangement', the marriage between brother and sister, through all ranks of the people up to the Throne. King Ptolemy II (285–247 B.C.), according to Pausanias, assumed for this reason the honourable title of 'Philadelphos' (that is 'sister beloved'), because, 'following the old custom, he had taken in marriage his beloved sister Arsinoe'. To refer to yet another special circumstance in regard to the ideas of succession to property derived from the earliest days of civilization, I would recall that Egypt was, under the Pharaohs, divided into numerous small counties over each of which a kind of county prince ruled. This dignity was not, 'according to old Egyptian laws', handed down from father to son, but (as the celebrated Egyptologist, Heinrich Brugsch, described what was to him the incomprehensible mother-right usage) 'from the father on the mother's side to the eldest grandson', or, expressed in other words, from the bearer of the dignity, through his mother, to a grandson of her father, who perhaps would be a nephew of the existing prince. Nicholas of Damascus, who lived at the time of King Herod (44–40 B.C.), reported a similar custom amongst the neighbouring Ethiopians : ' The Kings do not leave their thrones to their own children, but to those of their sister.'

I have dealt at some length with the mother-right question in order to show how the social position of the woman might have been powerfully influenced by the original conception of mother-right up till far on in historical times. Protected by reverence and often by religious custom, the woman was not entirely given up to the arbitrary despotism of the man who was growing more and more powerful in exterior affairs.

The rich and distinguished man was, however, in Egypt allowed to take as many concubines as he liked apart from the highly favoured chief wife—the so-called ' Mistress of the House '. In the palaces of the great we find, in consequence, the ' Women's House ', a ' harem ' apart from the main family dwelling. It sounds quite modern when we read in a papyrus preserved at Leyden, of the chief wife, who feels herself neglected, complaining that ' The woman tramp, who has become favourite, protects her father ; no one may injure him. She who has become mistress of the splendour sets her children on gorgeous couches; she who came without a petticoat is mistress; she who regarded her features in the pools now possesses a metal mirror. The concubines deprive the rightful holders of their property; gold, lapis lazuli, silver, emeralds and feathers, are seen round the necks of the slave-women, but the respectable women lament throughout the whole land: " Oh, that we only had enough to eat ! " '

The predominance of the Egyptian man is still more distinctly emphasized in the legal customs with regard to adultery. At lower stages of civilization, as soon as a man established a claim on a particular woman (by robbery or purchase) adultery was regarded as, judicially and soberly expressed, ' injury to property ', and degrading to the man's honour. Almost everywhere to-day amongst the lower races, only the guilty woman is punished, not, or only to a slight degree, the man. The punishment consists in sending the woman back to her people, whereupon her parents have to return the purchase price, in the payment of a more or less high penalty on the part of the adulterer, the guilty wife, or her family, and finally in the mutilation or death of the woman, and also, but rarely, in the death of the adulterer. In Ancient Egypt the nose of the adulteress was cut off (according to Diodorus), which, strangely enough, is exactly what is still practised to-day among the Apache Indians; or else she was buried alive, while the guilty man was only beaten.

The fact that the Egyptian woman, in competition with her companions for the favour of the man, employed every form of attraction, which could help her to the achievement of her amatory purpose, that of her own accord she came to lower herself to being merely a female, a luxury article, by her use of various toilet articles, cosmetics, all kinds of perfumery, salves and paints, new styles of hair-dressing and fashionable dress, actually led to the adoption of a particular goddess of the toilet, ' Besa ', whose diminutive statue was to be found in the apartment of every better-class woman.

All this reveals to us how firmly man, in spite of all mother-right influence, was able to maintain his social advantage. In the Papyrus Prisse the ' vicious ' woman is described as a ' collection of baseness ', as a ' sackful of intrigues ', and the prince Ptahhotep (about 3350 B.C.) in the oldest extant book of morals, gives the following advice to man : ' If you are wise, care for your house love your wife, nourish her, dress her and decorate her ; that is the delight of her limbs. Give her perfume, and pleasures, as long as you live, for she is a possession which should be worthy of her proprietor. Be no tyrant. Friendly conduct accomplishes more than rough power. Merry will be her breath and her eyes will be happy as she looks into the mirror. She will gladly live in your house and with joy and love work therein.' One can read between the lines that the original mother-right power of the woman, with all its sacred and age-long associations, had evidently been falling into desuetude.

Amongst the Jews of Biblical times we also find unmistakable traces of the former existence of mother-right. So, for instance, in the Book of Kings the name of the mother is always joined to that of the King : at the Royal Court the King's mother is conspicuously granted privileges in preference to the Queen. ' Therefore shall a man leave his father and mother and shall cleave to his wife, and they twain shall be one flesh ' (Gen. ii. 24), and this is repeated several times in the Bible (Matt. xix. 5 ; Mark x. 7 ; Eph. v. 31).

This means—and naturally it did not occur to the theologians in interpreting the Bible as they were not versed in the subject—

nothing more than that the man by his marriage (submitting to the law of mother-right) shall pass over into the family of his wife.

A few quotations from the Bible are particularly interesting in this respect, especially those treating of Abram and his wife Sarai, to which our attention was first called by the eminent historian Lippert. Abram sought to protect himself from the passions and rapacity of the Egyptian kings (Gen. xii. 11–13), and later Abimelech, the King of Gerar (Gen. xx. 2–16), by pretending that the exceptionally beautiful Sarai was his sister and not his wife.

By this statement he intended to mislead his superiors, who thought, as was at the time of the writing of this story generally taken for granted, that marriage between brother and sister was impossible ; and he did not lie, in that he, taking the standpoint of mother-right, approved from remotest times, by declaring to Abimelech : ' She is my sister ; she is the daughter of my father ; but not the daughter of my mother ', and she became ' my wife ', which could be allowed, as in this case the pair were not blood relatives. It seems to me that the first citation is especially notable because the author of the Biblical story undoubtedly did not know that in Egypt a marriage between brother and sister was not only possible, but, as mentioned before, was looked on as something absolutely natural.'

Among the Hebrews, however, whose earliest authenticated historical appearance on the world stage as the 'Habiri' or 'Chabiru', illuminated by the clay tablets found at El-Amarna (1400 B.C.), in which they are described as being restless, intrepid and warlike inhabitants of the Steppes, maternal succession and effective mother-right with their real consequences apparently disappeared quite early. A decidedly nomad people, living almost exclusively by cattle-breeding, necessarily stand under quite different conditions of life than settled agriculturalists.

As to the taming of wild animals for domestic use, this was the special task of the hunting male from the beginning: he remained also unrestricted master of the herds which pastured on the moors and multiplied without any particular care on the part of mankind. These herds gave him plenty of nourishment (milk, meat) and also furnished clothing from their pelts (skins and wool), and homestead material (leather, felt tents), and became a valuable, constantly increasing possession. These possessions, however, compelled the owner to seek new pastures frequently, and therefore necessitated continued change of abode. In order to guard the large herds, the man needed trained help that was well exercised in hunting and fighting, hence he was impelled to gain prisoners and slaves; and then he had to instruct his sons as herdsmen, and so it went on. It is remarkable that among cattle-breeding African tribes of to-day (as, for example, Zulus and Hereros) the women are never allowed to enter the cattle kraals; the chieftain himself, or his sons—just as with Homer's heroes—guard the cattle, and milking is almost exclusively the man's task.

Such important changes in economic conditions were also to alter fundamentally the social relations between man and woman. In the place of the maternal succession and mother-right arose the patriarchate. The possessor of the herds became the all-powerful ruler over all members of the tribe principally dependent on him for nourishment. He was compelled to obtain many helpers and consequently he needed women who would bear him many sons.

In Babylon and Egypt in particular this revolution in the status of the woman was evidently already facilitated. With the Habiri-

Hebrews, who settled down later, the decline of the matriarchate progressed still further, and from the point of view of our studies, it is here that, as the famous sociologist Friedrich Engels puts it, 'the historical defeat of the woman' begins.

The position of the woman in Israel, says Friedrich Delitzsch, the German Oriental scholar, after citing the contrary example of the Babylonian women, was generally recognized as humble from childhood onwards. In the Old Testament we scarcely find the mention of a girl's name which calls forth from joyful hearts thanks to Jehovah for the birth of a child, as is the case with boys. The woman is the property of her parents and later of her husband. She is a valuable labour asset, and in marriage has to undertake the larger part of the heaviest household duties. Apart from her body-slaves, she has no property over which she can freely exercise her right. Up to the time of the Babylonian captivity polygamy was practised. The man bought the woman, and the purchase price consisted often of strange goods, reminiscent of Indian customs, as, for example, that price demanded of David, when he obtained the hand of Saul's daughter Michal (see 1 Sam. xviii. 21–27).

THE SOCIAL POSITION OF WOMAN 111

Girls were excluded from inheritance in favour of their brothers; and, when no male heir was available, a girl could only have a claim on the estate of her parents if she chose her husband from the same family. In short, the view held was that woman's mission was merely to bear children and keep the household in order.

When we turn to people of the so-called classical times we must note an observation of Herodotus which is particularly apposite. The father of history relates that the Lycians, bearers of pre-hellenic culture as we to-day know, who had settled in the south-west corner of Asia Minor whither they had come from Crete, had the remarkable habit of naming themselves after the mother, and did not take the father's name. When one was asked of what family he came, he invariably gave the name of his mother, and that of the mother of his mother. ' When a middle-class woman cohabited with a slave, the child was legitimate; when, however, a middle-class man, even of the better-rank, had children by a stranger, or a female slave, these offsprings were considered illegitimate.' Nicolas of Damascus bears witness to this at a much later date, saying that amongst the Lycians property always devolved from mother to daughter, and not to the son. Here then we encounter matriarchal ideas held by a European race in early historical times.

We cannot wonder then that in the early days of the Greek civilization we also find undeniable traces of matriarchy. But these traces are for the most part found only in mythological heroic poems. Only in the Athenian statutes, where effect was given to the right to marry one's half-sister on the father's side—but not on the mother's side—and in the Athenian practice of full right adoption of the child of blood relatives (father, brothers and sisters) was the maternal connexion recognized and the matriarchal idea revealed within historical time. 'We marry'—so the orator Demosthenes once concisely characterized the relations between man and woman in Hellas—'in order that we may obtain conjugal inheritors, and further to have, in the woman, a true guardian of the house.' Love, in the higher sense of the word, was not yet understood by the ancient Greeks, any more than by the primitive races of the present day. The maids grew up in the female apartments (Gynaikonitis) near to the parent house, and as soon as they reached a marriageable age, and the parents had arranged the questions of business and household conditions with the suitor, they passed out into the Gynaikonitis of the bridegroom. Imperfectly educated at home, and in any case only instructed in feminine handwork and the needs of the household, without any connexion with the outer world, and especially also without that spontaneous mental development which arises out of natural contact and intercourse with the opposite sex, the woman, even as wife, obtained no mental advancement by the aid of her husband. In the heroic age, too, the conditions appear to have been similar : Telemachus sent his mother Penelope, on an occasion important for her, back to the women's apartments with the rather disrespectful words : ' Out, return to the apartments and take care of your business ; the spinning wheel and the loom, the command of the serving women ; be diligent at thy tasks ; the spoken word is man's obligation.'

When later, through political changes, the life of the Greek citizen became more public, the man was entirely estranged from his home, and likewise from his wife. A particular slave, the Gynaikonom, was detailed to guard and watch over the mistress of the house (in Greece also the wife bore this empty title) and in a certain sense to control her. Occasionally the master thought it right to close and protect the Gynaikonitis by bolt and bar. In general the woman, judged by the opinions of the old philosophers, was not considered of equal worth with the man, and therefore, in law, had no voice. That Doric and in particular Spartan women were freer, gives no ground for concluding, as some have done, that the women of these clans were more highly rated. The freedom enjoyed by the Spartan women, which allowed them to show themselves in public and to share in the interests of the men, and in the building up of the body by gymnastics, sprang merely from the desire to strengthen the female organism in order that healthy progeny might result.

Such a narrow status of the woman, and one so contrary to our modern attitude and feeling, can only, as the historian Bernhardy says in his *History of the Greek Literature*, lead to a state of debasement and depravement such as emerged so glaringly during the course of the Peloponnesian War (431–405 B.C.); the tragic poets (especially Euripides) give ample food for melancholy reflection thereon.

We see coming into prominence at this time a particular type of free woman who eventually subjected the masculine world. This was the 'Hetairai'. The 'Hetairai'

THE SOCIAL POSITION OF WOMAN 115

might be female friends, mates or associates, and those who are best known to us—Aspasia and Olympia, for example—earned for the class in general this honourable distinction. By their carefully studied and refined deportment, their allurements and physical fascinations, they lifted themselves not only above the common cocottes, but also overshadowed the Greek housewives, who entirely lacked those attributes of finer, better manners, higher education, and understanding of art, which won for the Hetairai, within a very short time, a definite influence in all circles of public and private life. The legitimately married woman, the ' Mistress of the House ', might protest as she liked, but she had only one weapon at her disposal against this encroachment—divorce—and that was two-edged. The married woman could press divorce when her husband brought the hetaira into the house. Pericles allowed himself thus to be divorced, and in spite of being a man of almost fifty years with grown-up children, he married the hetaira Aspasia.

Further passages from Demosthenes throw a strong light on the social conditions of those degenerate times : ' We hold concubines (slaves) for our service and needs; Hetairai, however, for the joys of love.' Such conditions it was that gave the historian of the Peloponnesian War, Thucydides, ground for his judgement of woman : 'If there is a God who invented woman, wherever he is, he must realize that he is the unholy raiser of the worst of evils.'

Prostitution, or whatever one may—in regard to the woman—care to call sexual intercourse between two who are not legitimately bound, had its beginnings immediately the common marriage took on a closer, more strictly bounded form. By nature the human male is not intended to be monogamic, and no ethical consideration can make it otherwise. Marriage forms are not fundamentally traceable back to any ethical understanding, but are the product of economic forces, and, further, of constitutional conception. Though the strong or rich man in the lower or earlier stages of civilization (such as we find to-day, not only among many primitive races, but also among adherents of certain religious sects) could have as many women as he could procure by robbery or purchase—Solomon's harem, according to the Bible (1 Kings xi. 3), numbered not less than a round thousand drawn from all neighbouring peoples, counting legitimate wives and concubines—the weaker or poorer man was in the position of having

THE SOCIAL POSITION OF WOMAN 117

to be satisfied with only one, or even no wife at all which he might call his own property. Even if this might not, from the standpoint of his economic situation, disturb him too greatly, yet, on the other hand, the desire for female society could not be suppressed and he would seek satisfaction by robbery or purchase. From such circumstances arise the origin and reason for that habit which in very different forms and designations became customary, and was soon considered as 'moral' (i.e. generally practised), or, on the contrary, as 'immoral' (i.e. not the practice of the people). Then it was looked upon as useful, and therefore necessary, until laws came into being which punished the practice as an offence against the state, and ultimately, wherever there are men and women, the institution is confirmed, and will continue, whatever form or name it may take.

The old Greek law-giver Solon (504 B.C.) had already tried to regulate prostitution, and founded a state brothel (Deikterion) to which any man, for a small fee (one obolos—about $1\frac{1}{2}d$.), had entrance, and from this rich and lucrative institution Solon built a temple to the Goddess of Love, Aphrodite, just as in later Jewish times the priests extracted a tax from loose women for the building of the temple in Jerusalem. The low Athenian trollops scarcely constituted a danger to matrimonial peace. A considerable change came, however, as Greece, drawing toward the Orient, came in contact with the luxury of Asia, and became acquainted with the free customs of the people there, principally of the hetaira type. Aspasia, already mentioned, came, like a great number of the Hetairai of Pericles' time, from Miletus, the Egyptian town of Asia Minor, and issued from the hetaira school of Thargelia. For her part, Aspasia, as wife of Pericles, founded in Athens a similar school, which continued for a long time and was attended also by the women and daughters of the Athenian citizens. The name of Phryne may be mentioned—who was recorded in marble by Praxiteles, and chosen by Apelles as his model for the 'Venus rising on the sea foam'—Phryne, who, out of the earnings of her profession, offered the Thebans a portion towards the rebuilding of a part of the destroyed city-wall.

Others, like Lais, Leontion, Theodota (under whose instruction Socrates wanted to learn the nature of beauty), Archäanassa (the hetaira of Plato), Herpyllis (of Aristotle), and many others are inseparable from the history of the blossoming civilization of the Periclean age. Among the hetairai we find mothers and wives of important men, and the brilliant lot of these woman—these ' Prostitutes ' socially elevated through their education, to call the child by its right name—soon attracted the steps of ' legitimate daughters ' in multitudes toward similar careers.

And thus the spiritual and artistic education of the woman in Europe begins with Prostitution. The status of hetaira must be regarded as the start of the so-called women's movement. Through it, as it reappeared in different cultural epochs in scarcely altered forms and conditions, woman loaded man with new fetters from which he has never been quite able to free himself.

The position of the woman in ancient Rome was in appearance only more favourable than in Greece. Among the Romans, too, the man was the unrestricted master, even though at the wedding ceremony the woman was handed a key as symbol of her domestic power, and the man drew an iron ring over his finger as a sign of his bondage. Often betrothed already in childhood, and already espoused at the age of twelve to thirteen years as the legitimate wife of a man whom her father had chosen according to rank and fortune, the woman had no will or say of her own, but passed from the guardianship of her father into that of her husband. But there was a great difference in the social position of the Greek and the Roman wife, in that the Roman wife was not placed in a 'harem' separated and cut off from everything. She shared with her husband his meals and his entertainment; she received visits and could leave the house whenever she liked; she might appear at the Courts as complainant or witness. The father of the house, the 'Paterfamilias', was really in the truest sense of the word the Master within the house, as he was its sole representative outside. The members of the family, so Laband, the famous legal historian, has stated, belonged to the Master of the House, just as much as slaves, animals, and goods belonged to him. At an earlier date it was not considered a crime for a man to kill his wife if she were addicted to drink, and the Consul Domitius once sentenced a woman to the loss of her marriage portion because she had taken more wine than the physician had prescribed.

Paternal right was already practised by the Romans when the Commonwealth was founded. This is distinctly shown by the position of the woman in the early days of

Rome, but, with the levelling up of these old conceptions of right, she improved matters to her advantage, and, in all spheres of life, obtained important concessions. She might now, for example, hold and control her own fortune; indeed, occasionally her influence was even felt in legislature, in so far as it dealt with matters concerning her own sex.

So it came about that the elder Cato (195 B.C.) complained publicly that 'Men everywhere else rule their womenfolk; we (Romans) rule all men, but over us, however, rule our women. If we had been prudent enough to maintain over our wives our right and superiority as men we would now be having less difficulties with womankind in general. Our lost freedom in household matters is invaded also in public matters and trodden on by the unruliness of women; and, because we can offer no resistance to them singly, we fear their combined power. When these unruly beings are given the reins of their ambitious and imperious natures, can one trust that any limit will be set of their own free will! To tell the truth, woman does not desire freedom but license in all things, and when she once begins to acquire equality with us, she will soon move on to push us into the background.'

With the penetration of the Greek civilization, and the growth of political power and opulence, the 'emancipation' of the Roman woman from man's control, predicted by Cato, made astoundingly great and rapid progress. All the manifestations of the Hellenic hetairadom now appeared in an exaggerated and degraded form in Rome. Later on, in the time of the Caesars, the wives of the highest state officials allowed themselves to be inscribed in the Register of public Prostitutes, in order that they might be able to satisfy their inappeasable lust without fear of punishment—for adultery, at least according to the Code, was still a heavily punishable offence—and nymphomaniac empresses, like the 'unconquerable' Messalina, surrendered themselves to all and sundry in vile brothels.

Such a conception of emancipation can scarcely be grasped. This female freedom made itself felt in higher politics. Fulvia was able to plan the Perusian war in order to bring her husband, Antonius (entangled in Cleopatra's net) back to Rome. The same Messalina, who sought her lovers in the lowest haunts from the dregs of the people, received in her palace foreign plenipotentiaries, and presided at State councils, ruling her weak-willed husband, Claudius, like a puppet in her hands. Agrippina was able to exert her mischievous influence over two emperors, the husband and son, and directed (profiting by the warning revealed in the fate of her predecessor in marriage and on the throne) the destiny of the world, while cleverly keeping herself in the background.

This gloomy picture of the times is scarcely lightened by the fact that many of these women had attained to no slight degree of education, and that their 'salons,' from about the year 200 B.C., were the centres of the intellectual life of the people, though an erotic atmosphere certainly prevailed in them.

One serious concomitant of the emancipation of the Roman woman, which was conceived as a striving towards ' higher things ', was the rapid decline in the birthrate. In the days of the Empire this assumed the character of a menace, and no laws, however stringent, were capable of improving a situation which eventually was responsible to a great extent for the decline of the nation.

Among the Britons, it is suggested by a passage in Caesar's *De Bello Gallico* (v. 14) that polyandry was in vogue at the time of the Roman invasion. Caesar states that ' ten to twelve men commonly possessed one woman, and indeed they were chiefly brothers and brothers, and fathers and sons'. Polyandry was, as we learn from comparative ethnology, brought about by the lack of women and the superfluity of men.

We meet with it practised to-day, by the operation of similar causes, in Tibet, among the Aleutians, the Tlinkit Indians of North-West America, and in South India, where the ancient epic Mahâbhârata, indeed, although describing it as 'unprecedented' that 'a woman should have several husbands', adds of the men, somewhat dubiously: 'They can never be at variance, as they all have but one common wife.'

According to Caesar's reports, the children of the common wife of the ancient Britons were considered as belonging to that man who first cohabited with the virgin. Polyandry gives the woman in primitive marriage an advantageous position, and one might be inclined to believe that many of the various rights which the old English law covered—for example, death of the man for violent molestation of the woman, a punishment which William the Conqueror reduced to loss of eyes and castration—were derived from such original advantages. Later, of course, the English woman lost in law much of her early superiority (see p. 129).

THE SOCIAL POSITION OF WOMAN 125

The Germans, when they came in contact with the Romans, were still a primitive people in every way, not long since emerged from the condition of hunters and cattle-breeders to that of settled communities. The reports of Caesar (in his *De Bello Gallico*) and certain significant observations (making allowance for patriotic embellishments) in the *Germania* of Tacitus, leave no doubt as to this, and we find in the sagas and in the customs of the Germans traces of the different marriage rights which corroborate them.

Polyandry was the custom revealed in the old 'Bridal night', which, as the so-called *jus primae noctis*, was maintained in Germany (also Scotland and Ireland) until modern times, and the 'lending' of the married woman or daughter to the honoured guest, for which the Edda supplies a convincing proof in the reception which the God Heimdall is given by three married couples who thus made it possible for him to become the ancestor of the Noble, the Farmer and the Servant. Such 'lending' can be distinctly traced until the fifteenth and sixteenth centuries.

The Edda tells us also in many passages that here, as everywhere, polyandry tended to matriachy.

Tacitus, in wonder, states that generally the

sister's sons and not the chief's were demanded as hostages, ' because the blood bond was considered as especially holy and of close connexion ', and, letting us understand the completed transfer from mother- to father-right, further tells us that commonly the children inherited, but when there were no children, then the brother, father and mother's brother inherited. Consideration of mother-right is further indicated, for Tacitus in Chapter VIII of his *Germania* says : ' They regard the woman as something holy and seer-like, and do not disdain her advice nor neglect her decisions.' In the same way we still (chiefly in Central Africa and in Micronesia) find chieftainesses and priestesses among many tribes who pursue the matriarchal system, just as among the Germans it is probable that, even in Tacitus' time, mothers and wives participated in the men's councils. Among the L'unda Negroes (Zambesi), according to Livingstone, the council was made up generally of women only, and the men never dared enter into the simplest contract or agree to render the simplest service for another, without the consent of their wives. Among the Bantu tribes the mother of the chief takes part in the men's councils.

The qualities which the historians, having

regard to the situation in Rome, frequently referred to with deliberate embellishment, as 'holy' and 'seer-like' in the Germanic woman were for the most part only the outcome of primitive traditions arising from the attitude towards maternal succession, which, to my mind, gains force from, and is explained by, the wonder of procreation and the secrets of gestation. This was the insoluble puzzle which for so long had excited the interest of the Ice Age savages of Předmost (compare p. 77 and Fig. 13). With this conception is also mingled perhaps the results of observing that in purely practical matters the instinct of woman—her 'divination' (see p. 66)—seemed incidentally superior to the intellect of the man.

We have, however, only faint traces to serve us in judging of these matters. Paternal right had long superseded maternal right, and what has been said of the Roman Master of the House (see p. 120) holds good also for the German. Wife and child belonged to the man. As Julius Lippert fittingly puts it: 'According to those fundamental principles of the old Indian Laws of the Man, so firmly and unswervingly maintained: the child belongs to the father, even as the calf is the property of the owner of the cow,'

The woman was stolen[1]—as Arminius stole Thusnelda—or bought, and the stronger or richer man might own several wives. Caesar reports similarly of Arioviste; Tacitus refers to it as being intentionally a kind of duty; and even at the time of the Merovingians, polygamy was the vogue.

Dagobert I (628–638), highly respected by the clergy, had three legitimate wives and numerous concubines.

The Canon Adam of Bremen (d. 1076) tells of the Scandinavians, the 'Vikings', that the men 'are not ostentatious and vain, except only in relation to the women, and in this respect they know no moderation. Each man holds wives according to his fortune, some two, three and more, while the rich and the chieftains have innumerable wives'.

That higher form of marriage amongst the Germans, praised by Tacitus as a symbol of the soul of the people, was but the 'monogamy of poverty', which is met with everywhere to-day where polygamic practice obtains.

---

[1] This was also the habit among the Celts, and the law books regulate the resulting right of possession. Children procreated in the first months belong to the family of the mother: they can, however, be sold to the father. In the secluded parts of Ireland the comedy of stealing the bride was still enacted until the middle of the nineteenth century.

Having bought the woman, so the man could sell her again, as Tacitus discovered amongst the Frisians, and this was still permitted in Germany till well into the thirteenth century, when in times of need wife and children could be disposed of.

In England, until the second half of the eighteenth century, the wife—who was regarded as man's absolute property—as one who dared not have her own will, could be publicly sold by the husband, just ' as a head of cattle '. Available documents show, for example, that a duke bought the wife of his coachman whom he fancied, while a bootmaker acquired the wife of a labourer who had been led into the market-place on a rope and handed over to the bidder of £5.

It is written that originally among the Germans the widow of the dead husband was ' given to the grave ', that is, the widow was killed, as I have suggested was the custom in the Ice Age, and as the discovery of double graves (see p. 75) might justify us in presuming.

Under the influence of the long contact with Roman cultural development, a gradual loosening of German legal traditions came about; the geographical position of those tribes living hard on the Roman frontiers resulting in their being affected much earlier than the North Germans.

Concessions were soon made on this or that point of custom, and ultimately the new conceptions gained legal authority. In this way the woman came to have a voice in the choice of her husband, and the earlier unrestricted power of the man was weakened to a milder state of guardianship (really 'mouth' or 'hand', the sense of which is preserved in the German word 'Vormund', or guardian) in which the right to kill was no longer recognized; the woman might hold her own fortune, even although she did not control it herself, and so on.

At the end of the fifth century the woman became in private right a 'person'. Then followed gradually the changes which, as we have seen, took place among the Greeks and the Romans.

'Feminine cunning encroaches upon the right which the complaisant man gives up. Many a justifiably free man became the property of a rightless woman; women were deeply involved in the destinies of states,' says the Germanist, Karl Weinhold, in treating of this change.

We find again, also among the Germans, the typical results of a too precipitate emancipation. Women played a fatal rôle in the fight for the foundation of the Frankish empire. The sociologist, Johannes Scherr, who surely cannot be accused of prudery, describes these epochs of the Merovingians in the following words : ' Obscene phantasy was vainly strained to devise new abominations and vices, which were natural in those princely circles. All, however, was surpassed by the enormities of the two kings' wives, Fredegundis and Bruniehildis, in whom was revealed what depths of depravity woman's nature can be capable of.'

The opinion of the poet and historian Gustav Freytag is similar : ' The worst German prince was restricted by his weak conscience ; the worst of these kings' women, however, as one must imagine, were quite free from this curb, and there was at times an abominable naïveté in their demands.'

The emancipated German woman differed from the Roman woman only in that in the southern woman sensuality controlled her activities, while, in the other, the daughter of a colder sky, the slumbering instinct of bestiality was uppermost.

It is historically recorded of Charles the Great that he had five legitimate wives in succession, at the same time maintaining as many concubines. We learn that two of his daughters, Berta and Rotrudis, the 'crowned doves', who flew nightly through the Imperial palace—as Alouin, the confidant of the Emperor, and late Abbot of Tours, warned his scholars—had illegitimate children, though this fact did not apparently disturb their father in the slightest.

Certain inferences about the morals of the Frankish nobility and people may be drawn from the examples set by the court, and the law books corroborate the opinions formed on such grounds, for they bear witness to the vain endeavour that was made to stem the moral decline. It is not even possible, from the suggestions contained in the secular and religious laws, to form an idea of the relations between the clerics and the Christianized German women of those days.

It cannot be said that in the first instance Christianity had much influence in raising the social position of woman. Influenced by the social conception of the Jewish race whence it originated at a time when political and commercial conditions were most intricate and susceptible to mythical undercurrents, it did not touch the critical question of polygamy so closely connected with domestic affairs. St. Augustine (d. 430) expressly condoned, or at least did not condemn, polygamy, and none of the Church councils of the first Christian century prohibited it as a sin. The Christian religion in general placed little value on woman, as may be realized on recalling the disdainful words used by St. Paul in regard to women and marriage, in his letters to the Corinthians. And one may remember those loveless and unfilial words of Jesus Himself, addressed to His Mother, ' Woman, what have I to do with thee ? ' not to mention the obscene expressions of later fathers of the Church, who saw in the woman merely an impure being, a vehicle for sinful lust. In such expressions we see not only the dislike of the woman, but very distinctly also the fear of the demi-mondaines, who, through their erotic arts and fascinations, sought to regain their lost power over the man.

That ultimately Christendom and monogamy became inseparably associated, is traceable to simple economic and social causes. Christianity has from the beginning been the religion of love, the creed and the hope of the poor and oppressed; and monogamy, as already indicated, is the natural wedded state of the poor and powerless even among people practising polygamy. We cannot greatly wonder, on a broad historical survey, that woman is devoted to this religion of the unhappy—this ' socialism of antiquity '—even unto martyrdom and sacrificial death. She interwove her life into religion, and fought for social equality : and for this reason we see the zeal of conversion as it developed among the Romans and Germans.

The shifts of the German against the pretensions of the converted woman are very interesting and sometimes amusing.

The change from polygamy to monogamy was not brought about by a restriction of the number of concubines; rather to the credit of the man, he made no special opposition to the gradually increasing importance and dominance of the chief wife. The important objection to this was, however, that the children of the concubines were no longer recognized as legitimate and entitled to succession, but were regarded as illegitimately born and without rights. And so it came to pass that respectable parents would not give their daughters to a man as concubines, and under this influence the monogamic conception of Christendom slowly established itself amongst the Germans. With growing power the Church was able to replace the previous economic conception of the marriage tie by a religious ceremony, and, as Lippert says, among the poor and oppressed,

THE SOCIAL POSITION OF WOMAN 135

who by force of circumstances were naturally monogamic, the new custom of marriage when raised to the dignity of a sacrament which gave them a higher standing, spread rapidly and effectively.

A new glorification of woman developed early, with the appearance of Mariolatry, which a far-seeing and material priesthood cleverly fostered. In the Virgin Mother the Church gave the masses a desirable object for worship and adoration, in substitution for the long-honoured heathen goddesses whose worship was generally sensual and licentious, such goddesses as Mylitta, Isis, Rhea-Kybele, Aphrodite, Ceres, Frigga and Holda, whose nature and attributes were rapidly assimilated in the minds of the people with the new worship of Mary. This is confirmed by many popular ideas and practices even at the present day. One can, I think, see in Mariolatry, which is based on the immaculate conception of the Virgin Mary, the last sign of that primitive uncomprehending astonishment at the puzzle of being before birth ; it is the last tribute of ignorant man in his deep-rooted acknowledgement of mother-right. Mariolatry, further, is not free from the erotic element. There are many representations in the Middle Ages of the Mother of God offering her breasts to a worthy saint—as in the well-known picture of St. Bernard of Clairvaux. It is not difficult to realize, says Johannes Scherr, that the chivalrous reverence of the Madonna was easily transferred to the whole of the gentler sex.

In this relation it is quite erroneous to suppose that the 'love service' of chivalry, and the idealization of the Romantic, reveals any platonic reverence for woman. On the contrary, the wooers of those times were attracted by the sensual element, and indeed may be said to have revelled in adultery. The change in the meaning of the old German word 'Minne' is here significant. The old word 'Minna' or 'Minja' meant originally 'hearty remembrance'. Later, this sense was restricted and twisted to an idea of sex, and gradually of sensuality, till at last—I am here following the argument of the Germanist, Karl Weinhold—its 'honourable sense in the chivalry of the Middle Ages weakened and it came to signify lustful pleasures and the worst forms of sexual indulgence, so that about 1500, the word itself was avoided as indecent'. It is always the married woman whose favour the Knight, himself not seldom a married man, endeavours to gain, by means of love songs of equivocal character or the drivelling

Quixotism of his ' Minne '. And the lady, not unwillingly pressed, responds with coquettish promises and advances just like the most experienced hetaira of Periclean times. The Greek hetairai condition was also approached, in that the ladies through artifice of dress and cosmetics endeavoured to give an erotic allure in showing off their attractions. At the same time, too, they were masters of good form— ' Morality ', or ' Mâze ' as it was named—and, thanks to their education by monks and to the instruction of experienced singers, they were possessed of much knowledge in the spheres of art and the sciences, in which they surpassed the majority of their adorers, who frequently could scarcely read or write. This experience in love matters, and ascendancy in education, oft-times in itself imposed some control on the wild desires of the men.

Moral standards in the citizen circles of that period—not to mention the peasants and people of the lower classes—were without doubt on similar lines. Aeneas Sylvius Piccolomini, subsequently Pope Pius II, has left a description of Vienna in the fifteenth century, in which he says : ' The people are entirely given up to the lusts of the flesh. The number of public trollops is very high, and, on the other hand, very few women are content with one man. It is common for noblemen to run after the beautiful wives of the burghers. In such cases the husband will bring out wine to honour the noble guest, and leave him alone with his wife. One says also that many women get rid of tiresome husbands by means of poison, and it is certain that burghers who will not acquiesce in the unchaste seduction of their wives and daughters by court officials are frequently murderously disposed of.'

Prostitution, in any form, is, as I have already said (compare p. 116), thoroughly natural, and therefore an inevitable consequence of monogamy. It is not dependent solely on the sex impulses of the normal man, but also on the unsatisfied desires of mature woman, when sufficiently strong restraining influences are not present. This factor is, of course, more potent when the number of women in a community largely exceeds that of man, or, on the other hand, where there are more men than women. But while with man natural compelling forces lead to prostitution, woman will seek to make profit from it.

In the Middle Ages these various factors tended to feed the swelling stream of prostitution which followed the introduction of monogamy, established by the Church by compulsory ordinance after a great fight, in which every form of relation between man and woman, other than that of lifelong union, was considered sinful and punishable.

At first the Church did not restrain her own servants from marriage; celibacy was imposed only on monks and nuns in the cloisters. In a decree of the year 869 it is set out that 'priests who hold several wives shall be unfrocked'. But within a short while the cloisters in many places had become pleasure-houses, and actually brothels; immorality grew beyond all bounds, the sensuality of the clerics being fostered by their secure and idle life; till Gregory III (1074) was forced by the infamy of the priestcraft to institute celibacy. The thousands of priests now sought satisfaction of their desires among those entrusted to their care, and under their control, as numerous popular songs, stories and witticisms of those times remain to attest.

In a similar manner morals were affected by the system of the medieval guilds, by which many mature males were condemned to a life of irregular wandering and consequently to unmarried state. Jealousy and fear of competition led to refusal of work to strangers from other towns, and the vagabond handworker also descended to prostitution for a livelihood.

On the other hand, unremitting feuds and wars decimated the men, and the crusades in foreign lands enforced the absence of the best of the male population for years. Large bands of men also undertook trading expeditions. In practically all towns, therefore, there was always a majority of mature females, and in consequence there came into existence ' Women Houses ' which were under the surveillance of, and taxed by, the lay and clerical authorities. The inmates of these houses were subject to special regulations, and they were in a position to demand strong action against interlopers, that is to say, courtesans not belonging to the guild. Not less than 1,500 ' errant women ' foregathered at the Council of Constance (1414), foreseeing good gain. In the army of Charles the Bold there were ' 900 priests and 1,600 prostitutes ', and as Messalina and other Roman Empresses behaved in the Suburra, so ' respectable ', Luebeck burgher wives in 1476 ' hid their features beneath thick veils, and in the evenings frequented the wine cellars in order unbeknown to satisfy their lustful desires in these haunts of prostitution '.

Prostitution in woman has always been regarded as a sin, no matter from what cause it sprang, though at times a somewhat pardonable one, as we note from the order of the Town Council of Nürnberg in the fifteenth century, which reads: 'In order to avoid various ills affecting Christianity common women were tolerated by the Holy Church'; and Luther from the first recognized the full right of woman to sexual satisfaction. With his sane, unimaginative materialism, the Reformer declared: 'The woman, when there is not a higher, very rare grace within her, cannot renounce relations with the man any more than she can do without eating, sleeping and drinking, and the other necessities of life. . . . He who endeavours to interfere in these matters yet does not allow their operation as nature demands, what does he want: that nature shall not be natural, that fire shall not burn, that water shall not wet, man not eat, nor drink, nor sleep?' In the *Tracts on Conjugal Life* it is set down that it is 'not a free willing or resolution, but a quite natural thing' that woman needs man, and Luther following this line of argument to its ultimate issue was probably supported in his consideration of the subject by the so-called 'Levirat marriage' commandment of the

Mosaic laws (Deut. xxv. 5)[1] in that he demanded freedom for the 'capable woman' who had married an 'impotent man', and desired cohabitation with 'the husband's brother or nearest friend'. In this sense also the counsel of Jakob Grimm, the well-known Germanist, in his *Wisdom from the Blankenburg Office*, was given to the impotent man, that he should go to his neighbour to help him satisfy the 'love desires of his wife', and should his neighbour fail him, then the peasant should take his wife, cleanly attired and richly bedecked, to the nearest fair, so that she may there find a lover to provide a child and heir. Behind this need of the woman for sexual intercourse, and such public adultery, there is undoubtedly the real object of procuring of heirs to the husband. In this one may see the visible signs of economic and patriarchal considerations. In this connexion, August Bebel, the famous German social leader, rightly emphasized the fact that man did not

---

[1] The Levirat marriage custom of the Hebrews makes it a duty, on the death of a sonless married man, for the brother of the deceased to cohabit with the widow until a son is born. There are parallels to this to-day in Punjab practice of the 'Niyoga', and in the customs of many present day primitive peoples (such as, for example, the Mongols, the Siberian Chukschis and others).

control his property but, on the contrary, the property controlled him. And from this point of view Luther's widely effective words must have been of importance in relation to the emancipation of the European woman in this direction. In truth the battle for the equality of man and woman was, according to the great reformer's view on sexual relations, decided in favour of the female.

It would be overstepping the boundaries of this study if we were here to endeavour to prophesy to what use, in what degree and how, woman will put this Lutherian idea of equal natural right during the coming centuries. Closely linked with such sexual freedom is, however, the inordinate irrepressible craving for finery, a further development and growth of those instincts which are in the street walker the marks of the animal side of woman. To satisfy sexual cravings, to induce man to choose her and take her, the single woman will think every measure excusable in order to distinguish her from out the ever-growing company of those with similar desires ; or it may be the effect of those herd instincts common to mankind, but particularly alive in woman, which lead to the use of supposedly effective and yet slavish allurement. About the middle of the seventeenth

century there came into being with the
'awakening' of woman, the word 'mode' or
'fashion'. We get a remarkable picture of
female psychology through the sketches of the
times, from which we note that the fashionable
dame took about seven hours of the day for
her toilet. We read in the memoirs of
Brantôme (d. 1614) what shameless measures
and what unbelievable means (compare p. 36)
were employed by the ladies of the French
Court in their endeavour to arouse the sinful
concupiscence of the men. In Germany this
female love of embellishment and finery increased immeasurably in the second half of
the seventeenth century, a quite unmistakable
result of the Thirty Years' War which, by
causing the death of so many men, accentuated the competition of woman for the fewer
remaining males.

Critical investigation reveals the working of
a law of Nature by which after a war of long
duration, in which the men are decimated,
the women unconsciously strive towards a
repopulation of the devastated land. The
World War of our day has again revealed this
phenomenon.

On the other hand woman, especially when
not blessed with physical and specific female
attractions, although mentally superior to her

companions, seeks to capture man, or at least to attain to a social position, through education and learning. Even in the Greek hetairai community, as has been several times mentioned, this attitude was adopted; it then passed over to the intelligent female world of Rome at the time of the Scipios, to the aesthetic-political salons of the ladies of the Empire, at a time when the education of the better-class women in the Middle Ages was cared for by intellectual priests. From the Middle Ages we have but few names of intellectual women of the standard of the Abbess Herrad von Landsperg (d. 1195), whose learning is revealed in her Latin *Hortus deliciarum*, a kind of encyclopedia for nuns. At the commencement of the Renaissance period (sixteenth century) there spread from Italy a custom of collecting a 'Dowry of Education'; as Gleichen-Russwurm the historian once humorously expressed it: 'The little Renaissance dame twittered in Latin and instead of fondling her dolls embraced Plato.' Of the thirteen-year-old Maria Stuart, educated at the Court of Valois, Brantôme enthusiastically reports that 'she could write poetry with ease, and I often saw her withdraw into her apartment, and immediately reappear to show spontaneously composed verses. Once she made a public speech in Latin before King Henri, the Queen, and the whole Court. In it she defended the right of woman to be educated; she put forward the desirability of woman being at home in knowledge and art'.

The blue-stocking type was *en route*, and found its first perfect embodiment in the maiden Anna Maria von Schurmann (d. 1678), 'the wonder of her time and the glory of her sex'. In the Schurmann drawing-room at Utrecht, where Grotius and Descartes were at home, that problem which even now has not reached satisfactory solution, was thoroughly discussed: the question as to whether woman was capable of attaining to man's achievements. This Schurmann answered (in regard to herself) by saying that only 'the perfectly-gifted unmarried woman, free from all other duties, had the right and the fullest right to demonstrate her knowledge'.

In England it was in the drawing-room of the Countess of Bedford until her death in 1627, that cavaliers and poets gathered round this interesting, high-spirited woman, and engaged in intellectual and poetic controversy. Drayton, Donne, Daniel, Jonson, were never tired of singing her fame in verse, she was praised in odes as 'courteous, facile, sweet', and mourned as 'a learned and a manly soul'. In the Swedish Queen Christina (d. 1689) there was, so to say, an amplification of the merely learned blue-stocking striving for mental domination; here was a ' mundane ' decadent, whose knowledge and spirit must principally be regarded as a contrasting background for eccentric eroticism. The seventeenth century brought a still further combination of intellect and eroticism cultivated by woman, when Spener, the founder of Pietism (1670), set his principle—religion is a matter of the soul—against the stiff letter of the Bible. This combination found its highest perfection in the perverse 'excitation' to piety and impudicity, such as the German Pietism which Eva Margarete von Buttlar, with her ' troupe ', brought on the scene later (1703–1705).

The emancipation of woman moved along all these lines continuously and was not to be restrained either by authoritative measures after the style of the Chastity commissions of Marie Thérèse, or by sumptuary enactments, or through the many efforts of intellectual men; for instance, the fine mockery of Molière, the sarcasm of Lessing's epigrams, the acid pencil point of Hogarth, or the malice of Lichtenberg. From time to time the different movements crystallized in remarkable personalities, well known in history. I will name but Lady Montague, and her perfect counterpart Lady Vane, original of the strange, adventurous 'Lady of Quality' whose memoirs have been interwoven in *Peregrine Pickle*; the Pompadour, the two crowned Katherines of Russia, Gravenitz in Wuerttemburg, Rietz-Lichtenau in Prussia, and Nell Gwyn in England, who played fateful rôles; the well-learned Gottschedin, Madame Necker and Madame Staël, Henriette Herz and Rahel Levin, the hysterical nun Emmerich with her wound-marks of Christ, and the Countess Ida Hahn-Hahn, types who lured many others to imitation, and as they still further advanced in philistinism, found in the philanthropic Mrs. Jellyby of Dickens' *Bleak House*, a droll mockery.

Political and economic crises and catastrophies completed the emancipation of woman in the nineteenth century, bringing about an equality with man in commerce. The woman who in the beginning worked for all members of the tribe and, as amongst most primitive races of to-day, was compelled to undertake the heaviest and most unpleasant work of the community as well as the particular household duties, such as spinning, weaving, sewing of clothes, soap-making, fire-lighting, beer-brew-

THE SOCIAL POSITION OF WOMAN 149

ing, and many other matters, was now through economic conditions driven, aye forced, to go beyond ' woman's work '. These changed circumstances, the new methods of industry, and the growing needs of commerce, rendered it necessary for her to earn her livelihood in those spheres which previously had been reserved to man. The successful battle of emancipation, dictated by necessity and the bitter fight for existence, began in Great Britain at the end of the eighteenth century. In the spinning and weaving mills and the fabric printing works there were working at that time, and for long after, often in unbelievable conditions, a hundred thousand women and eighty thousand children. As an illustration of this one may take the pictures drawn by Disraeli in his novel *Sybil* of the miserable lives of those children and women.

The Trade census of 1907 showed that 2,100,000 women were engaged in industry alone in Germany and practically 13 per cent. of these were married. In comparison with man's work, the labour of woman is unskilled, and for the most part mechanical, for which a lesser wage is paid. Here and there, however, we find conditions quite to the contrary. In particular in America is this so, and certain industrial towns (for example, in the State of

Maine) are colloquially known as 'She-towns'. There the men attend to the household affairs, the cooking, washing, nursing of the children, etc., in short, play the part of the woman 'because the wives can earn more in the factories' (compare A. Bebel, *Die Frau und der Socialismus*—The Woman and Socialism). For the rest the advanced position of the modern American woman, as G. H. Scheffauer correctly diagnosed, tends to a special form of modern matriarchate. It is a cultural survival of the conditions at the time of the early settlers, when the minority of females were able to exert their will over the males. This condition of things, which to the European is unnatural, exists to this day in America because the male members of the population are still in excess of the female (1910 : forty-seven million men and forty-four million women).

It is not my task to show here how the woman has gradually entered all cultural spheres on an equal footing with the man, how she more and more feels and thinks along similar lines, and how this economic emancipation of the female has influenced and changed all social conditions, in particular marriage. The evolutionary period is not yet complete. The 'Woman Question' is to-day, more than ever, in full flood. We have made acquaintance on the one hand with the 'suffragettes', with female University Professors, Barristers and Members of Parliament, and on the other hand the emancipated female has her 'crowning'—in Victor Margueritte's truthful sketch *Garçonne*—in the type of the feminine bachelor who, in one regard, incorporates at the present time all earlier emancipatory strivings. Woman has now in principle, if not always in actual fact (as Agnes v. Zahn-Harnack emphasizes in her clever book on the "working woman'), gained the fullest rights under the laws of all civilized people, as paragraph 109 of the Wiemar constitution demonstrates: 'Men and Women have fundamentally the same citizen rights and duties.'

* * * * *

In a book full of information, *Woman's Question and Feminism*, the sociologist, Prof. Dr. Wieth-Knudsen, of Drontheim, writes: 'Only the white man, that fair-haired, blue-eyed North European type, representing even to-day this race in Scandinavia, Germany, England, North France, North Italy and certain parts of Russia, offers his life companion an adorative esteem and an imperturbable faith in her value as a human being as well as in her kindness of heart. This phenomenon of psychic focussing of the man to the woman is quite an isolated one among all races and at all times.' And in citing my book for this, he refers to that speech of the older Cato which I quoted (see p. 121) and states : ' The moral of the modern emancipated woman and the dangers which threaten us men from this side can scarcely be expressed more distinctly than in these words which the Roman pronounced more than two thousand years ago. The fact must be borne in mind that to-day we are pursuing the same course and that we are going to meet the same fate, though there may be some time yet before it will take effect.'

And in fact : considering the ' feminism up to date ' which the senselessness of the World War has bestowed on us as the last product of a Pan-European diseased mind, one is inclined, in a final remark, to draw the attention of the man of to-day to the words of the old Roman Cicero : ' Videant consules ! '